WOMEN OF THE HARLEM RENAISSANCE ANTHOLOGY SERIES

This anthology series gathers short stories, essays, one-act plays, and poems by the unsung Black women writers who helped shape an era.

The series includes two types of volumes:

Short-Take Anthologies
Concise, theme-based collections under 100 pages.

Expanded Anthologies
More comprehensive volumes that expand on the themes or authors introduced in the Short-Take volumes.

- Texts are carefully transcribed from the original publications.
- Short introductions provide reliable historical context.
- Overlap between volumes is minimal, allowing the books to function as a continuous collection.

HalesitePress.com

FAITHFULLY YOURS, JESSIE REDMON FAUSET

STORIES, POEMS & PERSONAL ESSAYS

A WOMEN OF THE HARLEM RENAISSANCE 'EXPANDED' ANTHOLOGY

Introduction by
KAREN RAE LEVINE

HALESITE PRESS

Faithfully Yours, Jessie Redmon Fauset: Stories, Poems & Personal Essays
Second Edition

ISBN 13: 979-8-9923075-1-1 (paperback edition)
ISBN 13: 979-8-9923075-3-5 (eBook edition)

Book cover and interior design by Halesite Press.

Cover photo: Artistic rendition of Jessie Redmon Fauset c. 1924. Schomburg Center for Research in Black Culture, Photographs and Prints Division, The New York Public Library. Restoration and artistic rendition © 2025 Halesite Press. [Note: Fauset's necklace is the Phi Beta Kappa Key]

"Here on this desk is a book in which I jot down all the little, beautiful word-wonders, whose meanings are so often unknown to me, but whose very mystery I love."

—Jessie Redmon Fauset
"My House and a Glimpse of My Life Therein"

CONTENTS

POEMS FOR CHILDREN

TRANSLATED POEMS

EDITORIAL NOTES

Research for this collection was conducted over multiple years and drew on archival periodicals, newspapers, and anthologies published during the period of the Harlem Renaissance. Each work was carefully transcribed from its original publication and checked against archival copies to ensure textual accuracy. Spelling, punctuation, and dialect have been preserved as they appear in the source texts, except for the silent correction of clear typographical errors introduced through historical printing or scanning.

Selections in this series are organized thematically or by author to create focused collections that remain approachable for students, educators, and general readers. Editorial intervention has been kept intentionally minimal. Introductions provide historical context but avoid interpretive analysis so that the writers' voices remain central.

The introductions that accompany each volume are intentionally brief but are based on extensive research. They provide historical context and focused biographical information about the writers and the circumstances in which the works were produced. These introductions draw on both established scholarship and newly available sources, including archival materials and period publications, and reexamine earlier biographical studies. Their purpose is to illuminate the historical and cultural context of the works rather than to offer new literary interpretation. When literary analysis is included, it is presented through quotations from scholars whose work has shaped the study of Harlem Renaissance literature.

Source Notes

A complete research bibliography and supporting indices used in preparing this volume are maintained by the editor as part of an ongoing research archive and are not reproduced in full in this edition.

The editor also maintains a complete index of more than 200 short stories, one-act plays, essays, and poems that received a prize or honorable mention in the annual literary contests conducted by *The Crisis* and *Opportunity*. These contests were administered independently in 1925, 1926, and 1927, and the index is based on the published contest results.

Literary Contests

In this series of anthologies, each story, essay, play, or poem recognized in these contests is identified by a subtitle indicating its place or honorable mention, category, or special award, contest year, and the periodical that held the contest.

Also acknowledged is the winner of the 1923 contest for "Best Short Story by a Negro Student," hosted by *The Crisis* and sponsored by Virginia's Delta Omega Chapter of the Alpha Kappa Alpha Sorority. Judged by Jessie Redmon Fauset, W.E.B. Du Bois, and Arthur Spingarn, "To a Wild Rose" by Ottie B. Graham was the unanimous winner.

The Crisis

The 1925 and 1926 *Crisis* contests included Short Stories, Essays, Plays, and Poetry. In 1927 these categories were combined into a single award for "Literary Art and Expression," recognizing individuals for bodies of work.

Special Awards

- The Chesnutt Honoraria recognized the three best contributions published in *The Crisis* during 1927. In April 1928 the award was reinstated as a monthly prize for the best contribution, picture, or article.

Opportunity

Opportunity literary categories included Short Stories, Essays, Plays, Personal Experience Sketches, and Poetry.

Special Awards

- The Alexander Pushkin Poetry Prize (1926–1927) recognized the "most ambitious and most mature work of the Negro poet."
- The Buckner Award (1926–1927) honored works from any category demonstrating "conspicuous promise."
- The Van Vechten Award recognized the best story, play, essay, or poem published in *Opportunity* during 1927.

PREFACE

As I was exploring short stories by women in the early twentieth century, I came across a beautiful, insightful story by a Black woman I'd never heard of. Then another. And another. Each one was vibrant, original, and emotionally complex. As I looked further, I found the mountain beneath the iceberg—a wealth of remarkable short works largely unknown to mainstream readers and often difficult to access.

First, I had to reexamine not only my own education but the education system itself. In nearly all US public high schools today, the study of Harlem Renaissance literature is optional and left to the discretion of individual teachers and districts. But even that much is fairly recent. Before 2017, New York State's English standards didn't mention the Harlem Renaissance at all.

I'm fairly certain I wasn't introduced to any Black writers in my high school years on Long Island in the 1970s, and literature was only a small part of my undergraduate education in Engineering. But when I looked back at the literature component of my MFA in Creative Writing—earned at a progressive New York City university in 2006—I was struck by the absence of Black voices.

It was mostly by chance, and with great humility, that I came to understand the breadth of the exclusion of Black literature from the American canon—and the need for that to change.

As I researched and read the works of Black writers of the Harlem Renaissance, I found a deeper layer of exclusion. Zora Neale Hurston is widely recognized in that circle, and more women writers are slowly beginning to gain attention, but most of the literature of the era taught and celebrated today is overwhelmingly written by men.

This imbalance raised more questions I wanted to explore. A look at African American anthologies published in the 1920s confirmed the disparity—only 12% of the works included were written by women.* Still, I had my doubts, and that uncertainty led me down a path of research more intense—and ultimately more rewarding—than I'd anticipated.

I conducted an extensive study of the national African American literary contests held between 1925 and 1927 by the prominent periodicals, *The Crisis* and *Opportunity*. I was surprised to discover that 40% of the over 200 awarded short stories, one-act plays, essays, and poems combined were written by women. Women also authored half of the short stories published in these periodicals.† It became more and more clear to me that women were not on the fringes of a literary movement—they were actively shaping it.

I also examined the short stories by women that were selected for inclusion in post-era anthologies compiled by African American literary historians and editors. My initial survey of 18 relevant texts revealed more than 70 unique stories by more than 30 different writers.‡ To expand the scope to include poems, plays, and essays, I turned to contemporary discourse and collections by scholars Cheryl Wall, Lorraine Elena Roses, Maureen Honey, and others.

---

* *The Book of American Negro Poetry* (1922), *Negro Poets and Their Poems* (1923), *An Anthology of Verse by American Negroes* (1924), *The New Negro* (1925), *Caroling Dusk* (1927), and *Ebony and Topaz* (1927).

† Musser, Judith. "African American Women's Short Stories in the Harlem Renaissance: Bridging a Tradition." In *MELUS*, Summer 1998, p. 44.

‡ These were academic anthologies that highlighted only Black writers, were published after 1990, and included at least one short story by a woman written between 1912 and 1930.

I used the results of both studies as a foundation for building a meaningful collection of short works. I identified those selected for historical anthologies or recognized in the literary contests of the era as those most admired at the time. Works frequently reprinted in contemporary anthologies I marked as the most studied since. Through targeted searches of original periodicals and literary journals, I uncovered dozens of additional stories, poems, essays, and plays—some of which had never been reprinted.

But I wanted to do more than recover these works. I wanted to make them accessible. So I set out to create something different: short, approachable collections designed for students, educators, and everyday readers. That meant organizing my now-extensive collection into themed volumes that would resonate with modern audiences.

As a white writer and editor, I come to this work with deep respect and a strong sense of responsibility. I'm aware of the risks of speaking over, interpreting, or curating in ways that reinforce the very exclusions this series hopes to correct. That awareness shaped my approach at every stage. My role has been to gather, not explain. I've kept introductions brief and informative rather than interpretive.

It's impossible to completely remove the editor's experience from the selection process of any anthology. Every decision, from choosing a theme to selecting individual pieces, is shaped by what the editor knows, values, and finds compelling. That said, I've tried to keep my influence intentional, transparent, and as limited as possible. The process of curating each volume was guided by two factors: (a) my combined knowledge of the writing most admired during the Harlem Renaissance and the works most studied in the years since, and (b) a commitment to including all of the work specified by a theme, not just a selective sampling. For example, the poetry collection devoted to Jessie Redmon Fauset includes every poem she published between 1912 and 1929, including translations, children's verse, and illustrations.

In some cases, I took thoughtful liberties by shaping collections around patterns that emerged from the material itself, such as a volume of essays by writers exploring their experiences as women of color in the 1920s, or a set of short stories by six different writers, each offering a distinct take on the theme of "passing." For every collection, the criteria for inclusion are clearly explained in the introductions so readers can understand how and why the pieces were selected. This project is not about my literary scholarship. It's about helping to make space for these writers to be read, heard, and appreciated on their own terms.

This series of anthologies was created to amplify, not explain; to gather, not revise; and to invite readers into a rich, often-overlooked archive of brilliant and essential writing. My hope is that each collection serves as both an introduction and an invitation to read more deeply, ask more questions, and continue the work of recognition and restoration.

INTRODUCTION

As a writer, editor, mentor, and diplomat, Jessie Redmon Fauset was an essential, unwavering, and unsung force of the Harlem Renaissance. This volume celebrates Fauset's exceptional and often overlooked talent as a writer with the first complete collection of her short fiction, poems, and personal essays published in Harlem Renaissance periodicals, anthologies, and literary journals.

From the astounding gamut of Jessie Fauset's writing, this is a collection of her most imaginative work. Many of her short stories are precursors to her popular novels. Her poetry, in its traditional style, addresses timeless themes. Her expressive first-person narratives offer insights into the life and times of an extraordinary writer and visionary.

A LIFE

Jessie Fauset grew up in a household where money was tight and education was highly regarded. The seventh child of Redmon Fauset and Ann Seaman Fauset, she was born on April 26, 1882, in Frederickville (part of Snow Hill, now called Lawnside), a historic Black community in Camden County, New Jersey.[1] Her mother died when Fauset was very young, and her father, an African Methodist Episcopal (A.M.E.) minister, married Bella White Huff, a widow with three children. Over the course of adding three more children to the family, they moved to Philadelphia, where Redmon Fauset's ancestors had lived free from slavery for generations.

Fauset's education was a mixture of accomplishments, acclaim, barriers, and forbearance. Fauset was the only African American in her graduating class at the prestigious Philadelphia High School for Girls. When the all-white Bryn Mawr College refused to admit her, she attended Cornell on a scholarship as one of the first African American students. She graduated in 1905 and was likely the first African American woman elected to the national honor society, Phi Beta Kappa.

Despite her iconic academic success, as a woman of color, Fauset was denied teaching positions in Philadelphia. After a short time at Frederick Douglass High School in Baltimore, she transferred to the all-Black M Street High School in Washington, D.C. During her fourteen-year tenure as a respected French and Latin teacher, M Street grew to become the nationally renowned Dunbar High School.

Fauset's interests, however, were broader than teaching. *The Crisis*, the NAACP's monthly journal founded by W.E.B. Du Bois in 1910, was one of the first nationally distributed periodicals by and for African Americans. In 1912, Fauset had a debutante year at *The Crisis* with the procurement of the "What to Read" column, a poem, two articles, and a short story.

In addition to her continued contributions to *The Crisis*, Fauset expanded her world with travel and study. She spent the summer of 1914 in France—an expedition punctuated by the outbreak of the First World War. She spent two summers studying for her master's degree and, after a 1918/19 sabbatical, earned an MA in Romance Languages from the University of Pennsylvania.

Fauset's father had died on New Year's Day, 1903, while she was a student at Cornell. That same year, Fauset began a correspondence with W.E.B. Du Bois, who became a professional colleague and longtime friend.[2]

In 1919, Fauset accepted Du Bois's offer to join *The Crisis*. She moved to Harlem with her sister, Helen Fauset Lanning, and was introduced as the new literary editor in the November 1919 "Men of the Month" column.

During her tenure as Literary Editor of *The Crisis*, Fauset established herself as a driving force of an African American renaissance of art and ideals. She continued to wield the power of words on the pages of *The Crisis* in the form of short fiction, poems, essays, articles, editorials, opinions, book reviews, and translations. With encouragement, advice, literary salons, and opportunities to publish, she fostered the careers of many writers, including Langston Hughes, Countee Cullen, and Claude McKay.

Fauset co-founded *The Brownies' Book* (January 1920 through December 1921), a magazine designed to entertain and empower African American children.[3] During the magazine's two-year run, she was a dynamic literary editor and prolific contributor of stories and poems.

In 1921, Fauset was selected as a delegate to the Second Pan-African Congress, traveling to sessions in London, Paris, and Switzerland and reporting for *The Crisis*.[4,5] She was nearly denied a passport because as a Black female journalist working for what was considered a radical magazine, the government needed to be convinced, by references and interviews, that she was "a worthy citizen."[6]

Fauset published her first novel, *There is Confusion*, in 1924. It might have been that year that a seed of discontent began to sprout. In March, Fauset was slighted at a dinner at Manhattan's Civic Club meant to honor her and celebrate the publication of *There is Confusion*—one of the first African American books accepted by a white publishing company. Charles S. Johnson and Alaine Locke hijacked the celebration, turning the focus away from her to promote younger, up-and-coming male writers. The audience, expanded to benefit the "new generation," included influential writers and editors from mainstream publishing houses. Fauset handled the offense with dignity, but the anger she bore was made clear years later in a scathing letter to Alain Locke.[7]

In his autobiography, Langston Hughes identified Fauset, Johnson, and Locke as "the three people who midwifed the so-called New Negro literature into being."[8] The effect of Johnson and Locke's collusion at the Civic Club was the exclusion of Fauset from what Locke called the "cultural adolescence" of the literary movement.[9]

In October that year, Fauset left for an extended stay in France to study at the Sorbonne, work on her second book, and travel. *The Crisis* published five personal essays she wrote about this trip.[10]

Her return in 1925 was near the anniversary of her exploited book launch, and her disillusionment only grew with what she felt was Du Bois's dwindling interest in publishing literary art.[11]

In a January 1926 letter, Fauset appealed to NAACP activist and friend Joel Spingarn for help finding a position as a publisher's reader, social secretary or "to be connected to one of the Foundations in New York." She added, "In the case of publisher's reader if the question of color should come up I could work from home."[12] But none of these goals were realized. "Her varied experience with *The Crisis* indeed qualified her," notes Ann Allen Shockley, "but prejudices existed in the publishing houses more than ever..."[13]

That May, Fauset transitioned from Literary to Contributing Editor. She left *The Crisis* altogether in March 1927, taking a position as a French teacher at DeWitt Clinton High School in the Bronx.

"I found Jessie Fauset charming," wrote Langston Hughes of their earliest interactions, "—a gracious, tan-brown lady, a little plump, with a fine smile and gentle eyes."[14] A few months after Fauset left *The Crisis,* at a literary award banquet hosted by Charles Johnson, writer Eugene Gordon described her "pensive brown face and sad eyes."[15]

Fauset had stepped back from the publishing world but not from writing. She continued to contribute nonfiction and poetry to *The Crisis.* Between 1929 and 1933 she completed three more novels: *Plum Bun* (dedicated "To my parents, Redmon and Anna Fauset."), *The Chinaberry Tree,* and *Comedy, American Style.*

On April 3, 1929, Fauset, at 46, married insurance executive and World War I veteran Henry Edward Harris.[16] Their guest list reads like a *Who's Who* of Harlem Renaissance writers, activists, celebrities, and intellectuals.[17] Two of her bridesmaids were playwright and librarian Regina Anderson Andrews and pianist Helen Hagan Williams. W.E.B. Du Bois and Fauset's sister, Helen Fauset Lanning, acted as witnesses.

Fauset continued to teach French until her retirement, at 62, in 1944. She and her husband moved to a house in the New York City suburb of Montclair, New Jersey. She maintained her friendships in the art world and became active in her new community.[18] Two years after her husband died in 1958, Fauset moved to the home of her stepbrother, Earl Huff, in Philadelphia. She died there of heart disease on April 30, 1961, four days after her 79th birthday.

A LEGACY

From her first publications in 1912 to her last novel in 1933, Jessie Redmon Fauset's varied and extensive body of literary art encompassed the entire era of the Harlem Renaissance. She produced the most essays and novels of any African American woman of the time and was a prolific writer of short stories and poems for adults and children.

Yet her outstanding accomplishments as a writer and her significant role as a leader at the forefront of the Harlem Renaissance have remained largely overlooked.

The public eye is focused on Zora Neale Hurston and Nella Larsen as the foremost female writers of Harlem Renaissance short fiction. But Hurston is Fauset's only rival for the number of short stories African American scholars have chosen for comprehensive academic anthologies. The most frequently republished short stories by women in those anthologies are Fauset's "Mary Elizabeth" and Larsen's "Sanctuary."[19]

Fauset's short stories are a gateway to her novels. "In [short stories]," writes scholar Abby Arthur Johnson, "she experimented with the themes and characters she would later use in her novels. She dealt with 'passing' in the two parts of 'Emmy' and the three sections of 'The Sleeper Wakes.' ... With the two installments of 'Double Trouble,' Fauset penned a first draft of *The Chinaberry Tree*."[20]

Fauset challenged the norm by centering her stories around African American women in middle-class settings. She addressed themes of racial identity, self-esteem, gender restraints, class conflicts, and institutional racism.

In her poetry, Fauset expressed her worldview more intimately, sharing personal expressions of beauty, love, anger, pain, and playfulness. Her poem, "La Vie C'est La Vie," speaks to unrequited love and "Oriflamme" is a powerful and personal indictment of slavery. For *The Brownies' Book*, Fauset contributed many fun and adventurous poems for children. As a gifted linguist, she translated meaningful poems by Haitian artists from the French.

The spectrum of Fauset's literary skill is exemplified in the number and variety of her essays, including articles, biographical sketches, opinions, book reviews, and personal narratives. Her biographer, Carolyn Wedin Sylvander, writes, "Fauset's essays reveal a strong and gentle woman with happy childhood memories, an intense intellectual life and wide social contacts, a deep sensitivity to the lives of the poor and the foreign, particularly women. They also reveal a writer with wide reading experience, figurative and imagistic skill with words, and ability to make a point subtly and entertainingly. The personal essay form was particularly suited to Fauset's thought and writing skills. In a relaxed but attentive manner she explores in her essays opinions and experiences that are invariably forgotten in critical consideration of Fauset and her materials."[21]

Because of a decades-long, lava-like increase in scholarly recognition, Fauset's four novels have gained renewed attention. They're read and admired globally and included in academic curriculums. Unfortunately, her short stories, poems, and essays haven't received the same attention.

Contemporary scholar Claire Oberon Garcia shares an important observation: "The four novels represent only a small portion of Fauset's written legacy, however, which comprises dozens of book reviews, travel essays, journalistic reporting, translations, poetry, and short stories for children, as well as for adults."[22]

"An examination of the entire corpus of Fauset's work," Garcia continues, "reveals that she was concerned with exploring modern African American experience—especially women's experience—in a broad context that was global, modern, and cross-cultural." In a 2017 interview for the New Yorker, Garcia adds, "A look at Fauset's entire body of work reveals a writer who is more engaged with modern questions of race, class, and gender than she has been given credit for."[23]

Fauset lived only a generation removed from the abolition of slavery in a society where institutions, North and South, practiced inflexible codes of segregation. The government considered African American self-determination radical and dangerous and the battle for women's rights was in its political infancy. Fauset hit walls and broke barriers of race and gender every day and at every turn of her academic, professional, and personal life. Her accomplishments as a teacher, editor, mentor, activist, and writer, overwhelmingly vast and historically essential, were hard-won.

Scholar David Levering Lewis writes, "There is no telling what she would have done had she been a man..."[24] It might be more interesting to wonder if any of Fauset's male contemporaries, if they were women, could have accomplished nearly as much as she did.

Jessie Redmon Fauset wrote as she lived, with a unique and irreplaceable blend of intelligence, worldliness, strength, and grace. Insights for every reader can be found in the realms Fauset shared in her personal essays, created in her short fiction, and expressed in her poetry.

Fauset closed her 1926 letter to Joel Spingarn, "Faithfully yours, Jessie Fauset." As an often under-appreciated, sometimes spurned, and almost forgotten force of the Harlem Renaissance, Jessie Fauset's legacy of literary art remains, very faithfully, ours.

IMAGES

Fig. 1 Jessie Redmon Fauset, unknown date.

THE CRISIS

A RECORD OF THE DARKER RACES

Published by the National Association for the Advancement of Colored People, at 20 Vesey Street, New York City.

W. E. BURGHARDT DU BOIS, Editor
M. D. MACLEAN, Managing Editor
FRANK M. TURNER, Circulation Manager
ALBON L. HOLSEY, Advertising Manager

Contributing Editors: OSWALD GARRISON VILLARD, J. MAX BARBER, CHARLES EDWARD RUSSELL, W. S. BRAITHWAITE, KELLY MILLER

SUBSCRIPTION: $1.00 a year; 50 cents for six months. Foreign subscriptions, 25 cents extra. Subscriptions to begin with current issue or changes of address must reach us before the 15th of the month.

Volume Three APRIL, 1912 Number Six

CONTENTS

Agents wanted who ca

ONE DOLLAR A

RONDEAU.

When April's here and meadows wide
Once more with spring's sweet growths
are pied,
I close each book, drop each pursuit,
And past the brook, no longer mute,
I joyous roam the countryside.

Look, here the violets shy abide
And there the mating robins hide—
How keen my senses, how acute,
When April's here!

And list! down where the shimmering
tide
Hard by that farthest hill doth glide,
Rise faint strains from shepherd's
flute,
Pan's pipes and Berecyntian lute.
Each sight, each sound fresh joys pro-
vide
When April's here.

JESSIE FAUSET.

Fig. 2 Title page and "Rondeau," *The Crisis*, Apr 1912

In the April 1912 issue, Fauset shared her talent as a creative writer for the first time in *The Crisis* with the poem "Rondeau" (insert).

Men of the Month

Dr. N. H. B. Cassel Miss Jessie R. Fauset The late John Merrick

THE Honorable C. D. B. King, Secretary of State of Liberia and President-elect, accompanied by Mrs. King, have been visiting in the United States. In Washington they were entertained by the Liberian Consul-General, Dr. Ernest Lyons, and a committee of colored citizens. They were presented to the President of the United States, the Vice-President, the Secretary of State and the Chairman of the Foreign Relations Committee. In New York they were entertained by the Masons and a public meeting was held at Ethical Culture Hall. In Boston they were banqueted by the mayor and others.

Liberia College is represented in this country by Dr. N. H. B. Cassell, its president. The college needs an endowment of \$500,000—\$100,000 for buildings and \$25,000 a year for running expenses. Dr. Cassell has headquarters at the Church Missions House, New York City, and would be glad to give information to interested persons.

Miss Jessie Redmon Fauset joined THE CRISIS staff last month as Literary Editor. She has for many years been a contributor to our pages. She was born in Philadelphia, educated in the public schools, holding the alumnae scholarship in the High School for Girls, and afterward took her Bachelor's degree at Cornell, where she gained the Phi Beta Kappa key. She has studied in Paris and at the University of Pennsylvania, holding a University scholarship, and took her Master's degree there last June. Formerly Miss Fauset taught Latin and French in the Dunbar High School, Washington, D. C.

John Merrick was first a bricklayer and then a barber at Durham, N. C. He early began to invest his money in Negro business enterprises and became founder and presi-

Fig. 3 *The Crisis* announces Fauset's role as Literary Editor, Nov 1919

In the "Men of the Month" column, Jessie Fauset was, with a short biography, introduced as a new member of *The Crisis* staff and Literary Editor. As can be deduced by its title, it was rare for a woman to be included in this column.

The Brownies' Book

JANUARY, 1920

Dedication

To Children, who with eager look
Scanned vainly library shelf and nook,
For History or Song or Story
That told of Colored Peoples' glory,—
We dedicate THE BROWNIES' BOOK.

One Dollar and a Half a Year

Fifteen Cents a Copy

Fig. 4 *The Brownies' Book*, Jan 1920, cover and dedication (insert)

Just months after Fauset became the Literary Editor for *The Crisis*, she applied herself also as the co-founder and Literary Editor of *The Brownies' Book*. Many of her poems and stories were published in this magazine, "designed for all children but especially *ours*." Included in this issue is Fauset's poetic dedication and the poem "After School."

75148

The original and each copy of an application for a passport must have attached to it a copy of the applicant's photograph. A loose signed photograph of the applicant must accompany the application. The photographs must be on thin paper, should have a light background and be not over three inches in size.

Fee for passport, nine dollars. Fee for executing application, one dollar.

A woman's application must state whether she is married or not, and a married woman must prove that her husband is a native citizen.

[Edition of 1918.]

FORM FOR NATIVE CITIZEN

DEPARTMENT OF STATE PASSPORT AUG 15 1921 ISSUED WASHINGTON.

UNDER SECRETARY AUG 11 1921 DEPARTMENT OF STATE

UNITED STATES OF AMERICA, STATE OF NEW YORK, COUNTY OF NEW YORK. ss:

I, Jessie Redmon Fauset, a NATIVE AND LOYAL CITIZEN OF THE UNITED STATES, hereby apply to the Department of State, at Washington, for a passport, ~~accompanied by my wife~~

(Name and place of birth.)

I solemnly swear that I was born at Philadelphia, Pa., in the State of Pennsylvania, on or about the 26th day of April 1887; that my father Redmon Fauset, was born in Philadelphia, Pa. and is now ~~residing at~~ deceased

~~that he emigrated to the United States from the port of ... on or about ..., 19..; that he resided ... years, uninterruptedly, in the United States, from 1... to 19..; that he was naturalized as a citizen of the United States before the ... Court of ... at ... on ..., 1..., as shown by the Certificate of Naturalization presented herewith~~];

that I have resided outside the United States at the following places for the following periods:

England France, from June 1914 to Sept. 1914

that I am domiciled in the United States, my permanent residence being at 142 West 142nd St. N.Y.C. in the State of New York, where I follow the occupation of Journalism; that I am about to go abroad temporarily; that I intend to return to the United States within 3 months with the purpose of residing and performing the duties of citizenship therein; and that I desire a passport for use in visiting the countries hereinafter named for the following purpose:

~~England~~ (Name of country.) — travel (Object of visit.)

France (Name of country.) — travel (Object of visit.)

Switzerland (Name of country.) — travel (Object of visit.)

I intend to leave the United States from the port of New York (Port of departure.) sailing on board the Paris (Name of vessel or line.) on August 17 (Approximate date of departure.), 1921

My last passport was obtained from ... (Washington or abroad.), on ... and was I never had one (Disposition and number of passport.)

OATH OF ALLEGIANCE.

Further, I do solemnly swear that I will support and defend the Constitution of the United States against all enemies, foreign and domestic; that I will bear true faith and allegiance to the same; and that I take this obligation freely, without any mental reservation or purpose of evasion: So help me God.

(Do not execute before a notary.) Jessie Redmon Fauset (Signature of applicant.)

Sworn to before me this AUG 3 1921 day of ..., 19..

[SEAL OF PASSPORT AGENCY.] Elma D. Waldron, ~~Deputy~~ Agent, Department of State.

2060

[OVER.]

Fig. 5 Fauset's 1921 passport application (front)

Fauset traveled to England, France, and Switzerland for the second Pan-African Congress. Government officials almost denied her a passport.

DESCRIPTION OF APPLICANT.

Age: 34 years. Mouth: Medium

Stature: 5 feet, 2 inches, Eng. Chin: Round

Forehead: High Hair: Black

Eyes: Brown Complexion: Brown

Nose: Medium Face: Round

Distinguishing marks: Mole on right side nose

AFFIDAVIT OF IDENTIFYING WITNESS.

I, Helen Fauset Lanning, solemnly swear that I am a {native / ~~naturalized~~} citizen of the United States; that I reside at 130 W. 142 St. New York, N. Y.; that I have known the above-named Jessie Redmon Fauset personally for 34 years and know {~~him~~ / her} to be a native citizen of the United States; and that the facts stated in {~~his~~ / her} affidavit are true to the best of my knowledge and belief.

Helen Fauset Lanning (Sister)
(Signature of witness.)

Public School Teacher
(Occupation.)

(Firm, corporation, or organization, if any.)

(Business or professional address.)

(Do not execute before a notary.)

Sworn to before me this AUG 3 day of ......, 19....

[SEAL]

Elma B. Lewis
~~Passport~~ Agent, Department of State.

I desire my passport sent to the following address:

~~Rev.~~ (Miss) Jessie Redmon Fauset
Room 622, 70 Fifth Ave
New York City

A signed duplicate of the photograph to be attached hereto must be sent to the Department with the application to be affixed to the passport with an impression of the Department's seal.

Fig. 6 Fauset's 1921 passport application (back)

As with many documents, Fauset altered her birth date. It was likely to counter ageism, a common obstacle faced by professional women.

MISS LAWLESS, MISS WILLIAMS, DR. BROWN, MRS. JACQUITH, MISS RIGGS, MRS. LANE,
MISS McCROREY, MISS HOLMES, MISS BRIGGS, MISS CAUTION.
DR. BUCK, MISS SADDLER, MISS DERRICOTE, MISS FAUSET, MISS WYGAL, MR. TOBIAS.

Fig. 7 "The 'Y' Conference at Talladega."

This photo accompanied an article written by Jessie Fauset (seated, third from right) about a YWCA student conference at Talladega College in Alabama, where Fauset was invited to speak. Fellow speaker, Dr. Oscar Buck (seated, left) is holding a copy of the December 1922 issue of *The Crisis*, which includes Fauset's essay, "When Christmas Comes." The third speaker was Channing H. Tobias (seated, right), a civil rights activist and future NAACP chairman. (*The Crisis*, Sep 1923, p. 214.)

Fig. 8 Publisher's ads for *There is Confusion*

Left: "There is confusion. Holiday. Cane." *The New York Public Library Digital Collections*. 1925-03. Right: *The New York Times*, April 13, 1924, p. BR16.

MISS FAUSET

¶ Miss Jessie Redmon Fauset, literary Editor of THE CRISIS, sailed for France October first to be gone six months. Miss Fauset will study at the Sorbonne, Paris, travel and write for THE CRISIS. She expects to return in the spring with a new novel under her arm. "There is Confusion", her first novel, is in its third American and first English edition and is being translated into German at Vienna.

Fig. 9 *The Crisis* announces Fauset's travel abroad. "Horizon." *The Crisis*, Nov 1925, p.29.

Fig. 10 The cover of *The Crisis* by Laura Wheeler.

The April 1926 issue of The Crisis was Fauset's last as Literary Editor. The cover is by Laura Wheeler (Waring), a friend who illustrated many of Fauset's stories and essays. Waring's 1945 portrait of Jessie Fauset displayed at the National Portrait Gallery.

SHORT STORIES

EMMY

I.

There are five races," said Emmy confidently. "The white or Caucasian, the yellow or Mongolian, the red or Indian, the brown or Malay, and the black or Negro."

"Correct," nodded Miss Wenzel mechanically. "Now to which of the five do you belong?" And then immediately Miss Wenzel reddened.

Emmy hesitated. Not because hers was the only dark face in the crowded schoolroom, but because she was visualizing the pictures with which the geography had illustrated its information. She was not white, she knew that—nor had she almond eyes like the Chinese, nor the feathers which the Indian wore in his hair and which, of course, were to Emmy a racial characteristic. She regarded the color of her slim brown hands with interest—she had never thought of it before. The Malay was a horrid, ugly-looking thing with a ring in his nose. But he was brown, so she was, she supposed, really a Malay.

And yet the Hottentot, chosen with careful nicety to represent the entire Negro race, had on the whole a better appearance.

"I belong," she began tentatively, "to the black or Negro race."

"Yes," said Miss Wenzel with a sigh of relief, for if Emmy had chosen to ally herself with any other race except, of course, the white, how could she, teacher though she was, set her straight without embarrassment? The recess bell rang and she dismissed them with a brief but thankful "You may pass."

Emmy uttered a sigh of relief, too, as she entered the schoolyard. She had been terribly near failing.

"I was so scared," she breathed to little towheaded Mary Holborn. "Did you see what a long time I was answering? Guess Eunice Leeks thought for sure I'd fail and she'd get my place."

"Yes, I guess she did," agreed Mary. "I'm so glad you didn't fail—but, oh, Emmy, didn't you mind?"

Emmy looked up in astonishment from the orange she was peeling.

"Mind what? Here, you can have the biggest half. I don't like oranges anyway—sort of remind me of niter. Mind what, Mary?"

"Why, saying you were black and"—she hesitated, her little freckled face getting pinker and pinker—"a Negro, and all that before the class." And then mistaking the look on Emmy's face, she hastened on. "Everybody in Plainville says all the time that you're too nice and smart to be a—er—I mean, to be colored. And your dresses are so pretty, and your hair isn't all funny either." She seized one of Emmy's hands—an exquisite member, all bronze outside, and within a soft pinky white.

"Oh, Emmy, don't you think if you scrubbed real hard you could get some of the brown off?"

"But I don't want to," protested Emmy. "I guess my hands are as nice as yours, Mary Holborn. We're just the same, only you're white and I'm brown. But I don't see any difference. Eunice Leeks' eyes are green and yours are blue, but you can both see."

"Oh, well," said Mary Holborn, "if you don't mind—"

If she didn't mind—but why should she mind?

"Why should I mind, Archie," she asked that faithful squire as they walked home in the afternoon through the pleasant "main" street. Archie had brought her home from school ever since she could remember. He was two years older than she; tall, strong and beautiful, and her final arbiter.

Archie stopped to watch a spider. "See how he does it, Emmy! See him bring that thread over! Gee, if I could swing a bridge across the pond as easy as that! What d'you say? Why should you mind? Oh, I don't guess there's anything for us to mind about. It's white people, they're always minding—I don't know why. If any of the boys in your class say anything to you, you let me know. I licked Bill Jennings the other day for calling me a 'guiney.' Wish I were a good, sure-enough brown like you, and then everybody'd know just what I am."

Archie's clear olive skin and aquiline features made his Negro ancestry difficult of belief.

"But," persisted Emmy, "what difference does it make?"

"Oh, I'll tell you some other time," he returned vaguely. "Can't you ask questions though? Look, it's going to rain. That means uncle won't need me in the field this afternoon. See here, Emmy, bet I can let you run ahead while I count fifteen, and then beat you to your house. Want to try?"

They reached the house none too soon, for the soft spring drizzle soon turned into gusty torrents. Archie was happy—he loved Emmy's house with the long, high rooms and the books and the queer foreign pictures. And Emmy had so many sensible playthings. Of course, a great big fellow of 13 doesn't care for locomotives and blocks in the ordinary way, but when one is trying to work out how a bridge must be built over a lop-sided ravine, such things are by no means to be despised. When Mrs. Carrel, Emmy's mother, sent Céleste to tell the children to come to dinner, they raised such a protest that the kindly French woman finally set them a table in the sitting room, and left them to their own devices.

"Don't you love little fresh green peas?" said Emmy ecstatically. "Oh, Archie, won't you tell me now what difference it makes whether you are white or colored?" She peered into the vegetable dish. "Do you suppose Céleste would give us some more peas? There's only about a spoonful left."

"I don't believe she would," returned the boy, evading the important part of her question. "There were lots of them to start with, you know. Look, if you take up each pea separately on your fork—like that—they'll last longer. It's hard to do, too. Bet I can do it better than you."

And in the exciting contest that followed both children forgot all about the "problem."

II.

Miss Wenzel sent for Emmy the next day. Gently but insistently, and altogether from a mistaken sense of duty, she tried to make the child see wherein her lot differed from that of her white schoolmates. She felt herself that she hadn't succeeded very well. Emmy, immaculate in a white frock, her bronze elfin face framed in its thick curling black hair, alert with interest, had listened very attentively. She had made no comments till toward the end.

"Then because I'm brown," she had said, "I'm not as good as you." Emmy was at all times severely logical.

"Well, I wouldn't—quite say that," stammered Miss Wenzel miserably. "You're really very nice, you know, especially nice for a colored girl, but —well, you're different."

Emmy listened patiently. "I wish you'd tell me how, Miss Wenzel," she began. "Archie Ferrers is different, too, isn't he? And yet he's lots nicer than almost any of the boys in Plainville. And he's smart, you know. I guess he's pretty poor—I shouldn't like to be that—but my mother isn't poor, and she's handsome. I heard Céleste say so, and she has beautiful clothes. I think, Miss Wenzel, it must be rather nice to be different."

It was at this point that Miss Wenzel had desisted and, tucking a little tissue-wrapped oblong into Emmy's hands, had sent her home.

"I don't think I did any good," she told her sister wonderingly. "I couldn't make her see what being colored meant."

"I don't see why you didn't leave her alone," said Hannah Wenzel testily. "I don't guess she'll meet with much prejudice if she stays here in central Pennsylvania. And if she goes away she'll meet plenty of people who'll make it their business to see that she understands what being colored means. Those things adjust themselves."

"Not always," retorted Miss Wenzel, "and anyway, that child ought to know. She's got to have some of the wind taken out of her sails, some day, anyhow. Look how her mother dresses her. I suppose she does make pretty good money—I've heard that translating pays well. Seems so funny for a colored woman to be able to speak and write a foreign language." She returned to her former complaint.

"Of course it doesn't cost much to live here, but Emmy's clothes! White frocks all last winter, and a long red coat—broadcloth it was, Hannah. And big bows on her hair—she has got pretty hair, I must say."

"Oh, well," said Miss Hannah, "I suppose Céleste makes her clothes. I guess colored people want to look nice just as much as anybody else. I heard Mr. Holborn say Mrs. Carrel used to live in France; I suppose that's where she got all her stylish ways."

"Yes, just think of that," resumed Miss Wenzel vigorously, "a colored woman with a French maid. Though if it weren't for her skin you'd never tell by her actions what she was. It's the same way with that Archie Ferrers, too, looking for all the world like some foreigner. I must say I like colored people to look and act like what they are."

She spoke the more bitterly because of her keen sense of failure. What she had meant to do was to show Emmy kindly—oh, very kindly—her proper place, and then, using the object in the little tissue-wrapped parcel as a sort of text, to preach a sermon on humility without aspiration.

The tissue-wrapped oblong proved to Emmy's interested eyes to contain a motto of Robert Louis Stevenson, entitled: "A Task"—the phrases picked out in red and blue and gold, under glass and framed in passepartout. Everybody nowadays has one or more of such mottoes in his house, but the idea was new then to Plainville. The child read it through carefully as she passed by the lilac-scented "front yards." She read well for her age, albeit a trifle uncomprehendingly.

"To be honest, to be kind, to earn a little and to spend a little less;"—"there," thought Emmy, "is a semi-colon—let's see—the semi colon shows that the thought"—and she went on through the definition Miss Wenzel had given her, and returned happily to her motto: "To make upon the whole a family happier for his presence"—thus far the lettering was in blue. "To renounce when that shall be necessary and not be embittered"—this phrase was in gold. Then the rest went on in red: "To keep a few friends, but these without capitulation; above all, on the same given condition to keep friends with himself—here is a task for all that a man has of fortitude and delicacy."

"It's all about some man," she thought with a child's literalness. "Wonder why Miss Wenzel gave it to me? That big word, cap-it-u-la-tion"—she divided it off into syllables, doubtfully—"must mean to spell with capitals I guess. I'll say it to Archie some time."

But she thought it very kind of Miss Wenzel. And after she had shown it to her mother, she hung it up in the bay window of her little white room, where the sun struck it every morning.

III.

Afterward Emmy always connected the motto with the beginning of her own realization of what color might mean. It took her quite a while to find it out, but by the time she was ready to graduate from the high school she had come to recognize that the occasional impasse which she met now and then might generally be traced to color. This knowledge, however, far from embittering her, simply gave to her life keener zest. Of course she never met with any of the grosser forms of prejudice, and her personality was the kind to win her at least the respect and sometimes the wondering admiration of her schoolmates. For unconsciously she made them see that she was perfectly satisfied with being colored. She could never understand why anyone should think she would want to be white.

One day a girl—Elise Carter—asked her to let her copy her French verbs in the test they were to have later in the day. Emmy, who was both by nature and by necessity independent, refused bluntly.

"Oh, don't be so mean, Emmy," Elise had wailed. She hesitated. "If you'll let me copy them—I'll—I tell you what I'll do, I'll see that you get invited to our club spread Friday afternoon."

"Well, I guess you won't," Emmy had retorted. "I'll probably be asked anyway. 'Most everybody else has been invited already."

Elise jeered. "And did you think as a matter of course that we'd ask you? Well, you have got something to learn."

There was no mistaking the "you."

Emmy took the blow pretty calmly for all its unexpectedness. "You mean," she said slowly, the blood showing darkly under the thin brown of her skin, "because I'm colored?"

Elise hedged—she was a little frightened at such directness.

"Oh, well, Emmy, you know colored folks can't expect to have everything we have, or if they do they must pay extra for it."

"I—I see," said Emmy, stammering a little, as she always did when she was angry. "I begin to see for the first time why you think it's so awful to be colored. It's because you think we are willing to be mean and sneaky and"—with a sudden drop to schoolgirl vernacular—"soup-y. Why, Elise Carter, I wouldn't be in your old club with girls like you for worlds." There was no mistaking her sincerity.

"That was the day," she confided to Archie a long time afterward, "that I learned the meaning of making friends 'without capitulation.' Do you remember Miss Wenzel's motto, Archie?"

He assured her he did. "And of course you know, Emmy, you were an awful brick to answer that Carter girl like that. Didn't you really want to go to the spread?"

"Not one bit," she told him vigorously, "after I found out why I hadn't been asked. And look, Archie, isn't it funny, just as soon as she wanted something she didn't care whether I was colored or not."

Archie nodded. "They're all that way," he told her briefly.

"And if I'd gone she'd have believed that all colored people were sort of —well, you know, 'meachin'—just like me. It's so odd the ignorant way in which they draw their conclusions. Why, I remember reading the most interesting article in a magazine—the *Atlantic Monthly* I think it was. A woman had written it and at this point she was condemning universal suffrage. And all of a sudden, without any warning, she spoke of that 'fierce, silly, amiable creature, the uneducated Negro.' and—think of it, Archie—of 'his baser and sillier female.' It made me so angry. I've never forgotten it."

Archie whistled. "That was pretty tough," he acknowledged. "I suppose the truth is," he went on smiling at her earnestness, "she has a colored cook who drinks."

"That's just it," she returned emphatically. "She probably has. But, Archie, just think of all the colored people we've both seen here and over in Newtown, too; some of them just as poor and ignorant as they can be. But not one of them is fierce or base or silly enough for that to be considered his chief characteristic. I'll wager that woman never spoke to fifty colored people in her life. No, thank you, if that's what it means to belong to the 'superior race,' I'll come back, just as I am, to the fiftieth reincarnation."

Archie sighed. "Oh, well, life is very simple for you. You see, you've never been up against it like I've been. After all, you've had all you wanted practically—those girls even came around finally in the high school and asked you into their clubs and things. While I—" he colored sensitively.

"You see, this plagued—er—complexion of mine doesn't tell anybody what I am. At first—and all along, too, if I let them—fellows take me for a foreigner of some kind—Spanish or something, and they take me up hail-fellow-well-met. And then, if I let them know—I hate to feel I'm taking them in, you know, and besides that I can't help being curious to know what's going to happen—"

"What does happen?" interrupted Emmy, all interest.

"Well, all sorts of things. You take that first summer just before I entered preparatory school. You remember I was working at that camp in Cottage City. All the waiters were fellows just like me, working to go to some college or other. At first I was just one of them—swam with them, played cards—oh, you know, regularly chummed with them. Well, the cook was a colored man—sure enough, colored you know—and one day one of the boys called him a—of course I couldn't tell you, Emmy, but he swore at him and called him a Nigger. And when I took up for him the fellow said—he was angry, Emmy, and he said it as the worst insult he could think of—'Anybody would think you had black blood in your veins, too.'

"Anybody would think right," I told him.

"Well?" asked Emmy.

He shrugged his shoulders. "That was all there was to it. The fellows dropped me completely—left me to the company of the cook, who was all right enough as cooks go, I suppose, but he didn't want me any more than I wanted him. And finally the manager came and told me he was sorry, but he guessed I'd have to go." He smiled grimly as at some unpleasant reminiscence.

"What's the joke?" his listener wondered.

"He also told me that I was the blankest kind of a blank fool—oh, you couldn't dream how he swore, Emmy. He said why didn't I leave well enough alone.

"And don't you know that's the thought I've had ever since—why not leave well enough alone?—and not tell people what I am. I guess you're different from me," he broke off wistfully, noting her look of disapproval; "you're so complete and satisfied in yourself. Just being Emilie Carrel seems to be enough for you. But you just wait until color keeps you from the thing you want the most, and you'll see."

"You needn't be so tragic," she commented succinctly. "Outside of that one time at Cottage City, it doesn't seem to have kept you back."

For Archie's progress had been miraculous. In the seven years in which he had been from home, one marvel after another had come his way. He had found lucrative work each summer, he had got through his preparatory school in three years, he had been graduated number six from one of the best technical schools in the country—and now he had a position. He was to work for one of the biggest engineering concerns in Philadelphia.

This last bit of good fortune had dropped out of a clear sky. A guest at one of the hotels one summer had taken an interest in the handsome, willing bellboy and inquired into his history. Archie had hesitated at first, but finally, his eye alert for the first sign of dislike or superiority, he told the man of his Negro blood.

"If he turns me down," he said to himself boyishly, "I'll never risk it again."

But Mr. Robert Fallon—young, wealthy and quixotic—had become more interested than ever.

"So it's all a gamble with you, isn't it? By George! How exciting your life must be—now white and now black—standing between ambition and honor, what? Not that I don't think you're doing the right thing—it's nobody's confounded business anyway. Look here, when you get through look me up. I may be able to put you wise to something. Here's my card. And say, mum's the word, and when you've made your pile you can wake some fine morning and find yourself famous simply by telling what you are. All rot, this beastly prejudice, I say."

And when Archie had graduated, his new friend, true to his word, had gotten for him from his father a letter of introduction to Mr. Nicholas Fields in Philadelphia, and Archie was placed. Young Robert Fallon had gone laughing on his aimless, merry way.

"Be sure you keep, your mouth shut, Ferrers," was his only enjoinment.

Archie, who at first had experienced some qualms, had finally completely acquiesced. For the few moments' talk with Mr. Fields had intoxicated him. The vision of work, plenty of it, his own chosen kind—and the opportunity to do it as a man—not an exception, but as a plain ordinary man among other men—was too much for him.

"It was my big chance, Emmy," he told her one day. He was spending his brief vacation in Plainville, and the two, having talked themselves out on other things, had returned to their old absorbing topic. He went on a little pleadingly, for she had protested. "I couldn't resist it. You don't know what it means to me. I don't care about being white in itself any more than you do—but I do care about a white man's chances. Don't let's talk about it any more though; here it's the first week in September and I have to go the 15th. I may not he back till Christmas. I should hate to think that you—you were changed toward me, Emmy."

"I'm not changed, Archie," she assured him gravely, "only somehow it makes me feel that you're different. I can't quite look up to you as I used. I don't like the idea of considering the end justified by the means."

She was silent, watching the falling leaves flutter like golden butterflies against her white dress. As she stood there in the old-fashioned garden, she seemed to the boy's adoring eyes like some beautiful but inflexible bronze goddess.

"I couldn't expect you to look up to me, Emmy, as though I were on a pedestal," he began miserably, "but I do want you to respect me, because—oh, Emmy, don't you see? I love you very much and I hope you will—I want you to—oh, Emmy, couldn't you like me a little? I—I've never thought ever of anyone but you. I didn't mean to tell you all about this now—I meant to wait until I really was successful, and then come and lay it all at your beautiful feet. You're so lovely, Emmy. But if you despise me—" he was very humble.

For once in her calm young life Emmy was completely surprised. But she had to get to the root of things. "You mean," she faltered, "you mean you want"—she couldn't say it.

"I mean I want you to marry me," he said, gaining courage from her confusion. "Oh, have I frightened you, Emmy, dearest—of course you couldn't like me well enough for that all in a heap—it's different with me. I've always loved you, Emmy. But if you'd only think about it."

"Oh," she breathed, "there's Céleste. Oh, Archie, I don't know, it's all so funny. And we're so young. I couldn't really tell anything about my feelings anyway—you know, I've never seen anybody but you." Then as his face clouded—"Oh, well, I guess even if I had I wouldn't like him any better. Yes, Céleste, we're coming in. Archie, mother says you're to have dinner with us every night you're here, if you can."

There was no more said about the secret that Archie was keeping from Mr. Fields. There were too many other things to talk about—reasons why he had always loved Emmy; reasons why she couldn't be sure just yet; reasons why, if she were sure, she couldn't say yes.

Archie hung between high hope and despair, while Emmy, it must be confessed, enjoyed herself, albeit innocently enough, and grew distractingly pretty. On the last day as they sat in the sitting room, gaily recounting childish episodes, Archie suddenly asked her again. He was so grave and serious that she really became frightened.

"Oh, Archie, I couldn't—I don't really want to. It's so lovely just being a girl. I think I do like you—of course I like you lots. But couldn't we just be friends and keep going on—so?"

"No," he told her harshly, his face set and miserable; "no, we can't. And, Emmy—I'm not coming back any more—I couldn't stand it." His voice broke, he was fighting to keep back the hot boyish tears. After all he was only 21. "I'm sorry I troubled you," he said proudly.

She looked at him pitifully. "I don't want you to go away forever, Archie," she said tremulously. She made no effort to keep back the tears. "I've been so lonely this last year since I've been out of school—you can't think."

He was down on his knees, his arms around her. "Emmy, Emmy, look up—are you crying for me, dear? Do you want me to come back—you do—you mean it? Emmy, you must love me, you do—a little." He kissed her slim fingers.

"Are you going to marry me? Look at me, Emmy—you

are! Oh, Emmy, do you know I'm—I'm going to kiss you."

The stage came lumbering up not long afterward, and bore him away to the train—triumphant and absolutely happy.

"My heart," sang Emmy rapturously as she ran up the broad, old-fashioned stairs to her room—"my heart is like a singing bird."

IV.

The year that followed seemed to her perfection. Archie's letters alone would have made it that. Emmy was quite sure that there had never been any other letters like them. She used to read them aloud to her mother.

Not all of them, though, for some were too precious for any eye but her own. She used to pore over them alone in her room at night, planning to answer them with an abandon equal to his own, but always finally evolving the same shy, almost timid epistle, which never failed to awaken in her lover's breast a sense equally of amusement and reverence. Her shyness seemed to him the most exquisite thing in the world—so exquisite, indeed, that he almost wished it would never vanish, were it not that its very disappearance would be the measure of her trust in him. His own letters showed plainly his adoration.

Only once had a letter of his caused a fleeting pang of misapprehension. He had been speaking of the persistent good fortune which had been his in Philadelphia.

"You can't think how lucky I am any way," the letter ran on. "The other day I was standing on the corner of Fourth and Chestnut Streets at noon —you ought to see Chestnut Street at 12 o'clock, Emmy—and someone came up, looked at me and said: 'Well, if it isn't Archie Ferrers!' And guess who it was, Emmy? Do you remember the Higginses who used to live over in Newtown? I don't suppose you ever knew them, only they were so queer looking that you must recall them. They were all sorts of colors from black with 'good' hair to yellow with the red, kinky kind. And then there was Maude, clearly a Higgins, and yet not looking like any of them, you know; perfectly white, with blue eyes and fair hair. Well, this was Maude, and, say, maybe she didn't look good. I couldn't tell you what she had on, but it was all right, and I was glad to take her over to the Reading Terminal and put her on a train to New York.

"I guess you're wondering where my luck is in all this tale, but you wait. Just as we started up the stairs of the depot, whom should we run into but young Peter Fields, my boss's son and heir, you know. Really, I thought I'd faint, and then I remembered that Maude was whiter than he in looks, and that there was nothing to give me away. He wanted to talk to us, but I hurried her off to her train. You know, it's a queer thing, Emmy; some girls are just naturally born stylish. Now there are both you and Maude Higgins, brought up from little things in a tiny inland town, and both of you able to give any of these city girls all sorts of odds in the matter of dressing."

Emmy put the letter down, wondering what had made her grow so cold.

"I wonder," she mused. She turned and looked in the glass to be confronted by a charming vision, slender—and dusky.

"ARCHIE LOVES YOU, GIRL," SHE SAID TO THE FACE IN THE GLASS.

"I am black," she thought, "but comely." She laughed to herself happily. "Archie loves you, girl," she said to the face in the glass, and put the little fear behind her. It met her insistently now and then, however, until the next week brought a letter begging her to get her mother to bring her to Philadelphia for a week or so.

"I can't get off till Thanksgiving, dearest, and I'm so lonely and disappointed. You know, I had looked forward so to spending the 15th of September with you—do you remember that date, sweetheart? I wouldn't have you come now in all this heat—you can't imagine how hot Philadelphia is, Emmy—but it's beautiful here in October. You'll love it, Emmy. It's such a big city—miles and miles of long, narrow streets, rather ugly, too, but all so interesting. You'll like Chestnut and Market Streets, where the big shops are, and South Street, teeming with Jews and colored people, though there are more of these last on Lombard Street. You never dreamed of so many colored people, Emmy Carrel—or such kinds.

"And then there are the parks and the theatres, and music and restaurants. And Broad Street late at night, all silent with gold, electric lights beckoning you on for miles and miles. Do you think your mother will let me take you out by yourself, Emmy? You'd be willing, wouldn't you?"

If Emmy needed more reassurance than that she received it when Archie, a month later, met her and her mother at Broad Street station in Philadelphia. The boy was radiant. Mrs. Carrel, too, put aside her usual reticence, and the three were in fine spirits by the time they reached the rooms which Archie had procured for them on Christian Street. Once ensconced, the older woman announced her intention of taking advantage of the stores.

"I shall be shopping practically all day," she informed them. "I'll be so tired in the afternoons and evenings, Archie, that I'll have to get you to take my daughter off my hands."

Her daughter was delighted, but not more transparently so than her appointed cavalier. He was overjoyed at the thought of playing host and of showing Emmy the delights of city life.

"By the time I've finished showing you one-fifth of what I've planned you'll give up the idea of waiting 'way till next October and marry me Christmas. Say, do it anyway, Emmy, won't you?" He waited tensely, but she only shook her head.

"Oh, I couldn't, Archie, and anyway you must show me first your wonderful city."

They did manage to cover a great deal of ground, though their mutual absorption made its impression on them very doubtful. Some things though Emmy never forgot. There was a drive one wonderful, golden October afternoon along the Wissahickon. Emmy, in her perfectly correct gray suit and smart little gray hat, held the reins—in, itself a sort of measure of Archie's devotion to her, for he was wild about horses. He sat beside her ecstatic, ringing all the changes from a boy's nonsense to the most mature kind of seriousness. And always he looked at her with his passionate though reverent eyes. They were very happy.

There was some wonderful music, too, at the Academy. That was by accident though. For they had started for the theatre—had reached there in fact. The usher was taking the tickets.

"This way, Emmy," said Archie. The usher looked up aimlessly, then, as his eyes traveled from the seeming young foreigner to the colored girl beside him, he flushed a little.

"Is the young lady with you?" he whispered politely enough. But Emmy, engrossed in a dazzling vision in a pink décolleté gown, would not in any event have heard him.

"She is," responded Archie alertly. "What's the trouble, isn't to-night the 17th?"

The usher passed over this question with another—who had bought the tickets? Archie of course had, and told him so, frankly puzzled.

"I see. Well, I'm sorry," the man said evenly, "but these seats are already occupied, and the rest of the floor is sold out besides. There's a mistake somewhere. Now if you'll take these tickets back to the office I can promise you they'll give you the best seats left in the balcony."

"What's the matter?" asked Emmy, tearing her glance from the pink vision at last. "Oh, Archie, you're hurting my arm; don't hold it that tight. Why—why are we going away from the theatre? Oh, Archie, are you sick? You're just as white!"

"There was some mistake about the tickets," he got out, trying to keep his voice steady. "And a fellow in the crowd gave me an awful dig just then; guess that's why I'm pale. I'm so sorry, Emmy—I was so stupid, it's all my fault."

"What was the matter with the tickets?" she asked, incuriously. "That's the Bellevue-Stratford over there, isn't it? Then the Academy of Music must be near here. See how fast I'm learning? Let's go there; I've never heard a symphony concert. And, Archie, I've always heard that the best way to hear big music like that is at a distance, so get gallery tickets."

He obeyed her, fearful that if there were any trouble this time she might hear it. Emmy enjoyed it all thoroughly, wondering a little, however, at his silence. "I guess he's tired," she thought. She would have been amazed to know his thoughts as he sat there staring moodily at the orchestra. "This damnation color business," he kept saying over and over.

That night as they stood in the vestibule of the Christian Street house Emmy, for the first time, volunteered him a kiss. "Such a nice, tired boy," she said gently. Afterward he stood for a long time bareheaded on the steps looking at the closed door. Nothing he felt could crush him as much as that kiss had lifted him up.

V.

Not even for lovers can a week last forever. Archie had kept till the last day what he considered his choicest bit of exploring. This was to take Emmy down into old Philadelphia and show her how the city had grown up from the waterfront—and by means of what tortuous self-governing streets. It was a sight at once dear and yet painful to his methodical, mathematical mind. They had explored Dock and Beach Streets, and had got over into Shackamaxon, where he showed her Penn Treaty Park, and they had sat in the little pavilion overlooking the Delaware.

Not many colored people came through this vicinity, and the striking pair caught many a wondering, as well as admiring, glance. They caught, too, the aimless, wandering eye of Mr. Nicholas Fields as he lounged, comfortably smoking, on the rear of a "Gunner's Run" car, on his way to Shackamaxon Ferry. Something in the young fellow's walk seemed vaguely familiar to him, and he leaned way out toward the sidewalk to see who that he knew could be over in this cheerless, forsaken locality.

"Gad!" he said to himself in surprise, "if it isn't young Ferrers, with a lady, too! Hello, why it's a colored woman! Ain't he a rip? Always thought he seemed too proper. Got her dressed to death, too; so that's how his money goes!" He dismissed the matter with a smile and a shrug of his shoulders.

Perhaps he would never have thought of it again had not Archie, rushing into the office a trifle late the next morning, caromed directly into him.

"Oh, it's you," he said, receiving his clerk's smiling apology. "What d'you mean by knocking into anybody like that?" Mr. Fields was facetious with his favorite employees. "Evidently your Shackamaxon trip upset you a little. Where'd you get your black Venus, my boy? I'll bet you don't have one cent to rub against another at the end of a month. Oh, you needn't get red; boys will be boys, and everyone to his taste. Clarkson," he broke off, crossing to his secretary, "if Mr. Hunter calls me up, hold the phone and send over to the bank for me."

He had gone, and Archie, white now and shaken, entered his own little room. He sat down at the desk and sank his head in his hands. It had taken a moment for the insult to Emmy to sink in, but even when it did the thought of his own false position had held him back. The shame of it bit into him. "I'm a coward," he said to himself, staring miserably at the familiar wall. "I'm a wretched cad to let him think that of Emmy—Emmy! and she the whitest angel that ever lived, purity incarnate." His cowardice made him sick. "I'll go and tell him," he said, and started for the door.

"If you do," whispered common sense, "you'll lose your job and then what would become of you? After all Emmy need never know."

"But I'll always know I didn't defend her," he answered back silently.

"He's gone out to the bank anyhow," went on the inward opposition. "What's the use of rushing in there and telling him before the whole board of directors?"

"Well, then, when he comes back," he capitulated, but he felt himself weaken.

But Mr. Fields didn't come back. When Mr. Hunter called him up, Clarkson connected him with the bank, with the result that Mr. Fields left for Reading in the course of an hour. He didn't come back for a week.

Meanwhile Archie tasted the depths of self-abasement. "But what am I to do?" he groaned to himself at nights. "If I tell him I'm colored he'll kick me out, and if I go anywhere else I'd run the same risk. If I'd only knocked him down! After all she'll never know and I'll make it up to her. I'll be so good to her—dear little Emmy! But how could I know that he would take that view of it—beastly low mind he must have!" He colored up like a girl at the thought of it.

He passed the week thus, alternately reviling and defending himself. He knew now though that he would never have the courage to tell. The economy of the thing he decided was at least as important as the principle. And always he wrote to Emmy letters of such passionate adoration that the girl for all her natural steadiness was carried off her feet.

"How he loves me," she thought happily. "If mother is willing I believe—yes, I will—I'll marry him Christmas. But I won't tell him till he comes Thanksgiving."

When Mr. Fields came back he sent immediately for his son Peter. The two held some rather stormy consultations, which were renewed for several days. Peter roomed in town, while his father lived out at Chestnut Hill. Eventually Archie was sent for.

"You're not looking very fit, my boy." Mr. Fields greeted him kindly; "working too hard I suppose over those specifications. Well, here's a tonic for you. This last week has shown me that I need someone younger than myself to take a hand in the business. I'm getting too old or too tired or something. Anyhow, I'm played out.

"I've tried to make this young man here,—with an angry glance at his son—"see that the mantle ought to fall on him, but he won't hear of it. Says the business can stop for all he cares; he's got enough money anyway. Gad, in my day young men liked to work, instead of dabbling around in this filthy social settlement business—with a lot of old maids."

Peter smiled contentedly. "Sally in our alley, what?" he put in diabolically. The older man glared at him, exasperated.

"Now look here, Ferrers," he went on abruptly. "I've had my eye on you ever since you first came. I don't know a thing about you outside of Mr. Fallon's recommendation, but I can see you've got good stuff in you—and what's more, you're a born engineer. If you had some money, I'd take you into partnership at once, but I believe you told me that all you had was your salary." Archie nodded.

"Well, now, I tell you what I'm going to do. I'm going to take you in as a sort of silent partner, teach you the business end of the concern, and in the course of a few years, place the greater part of the management in your hands. You can see you won't lose by it. Of course I'll still be head, and after I step out Peter will take my place, though only nominally I suppose."

He sighed; his son's business defection was a bitter point with him. But that imperturbable young man only nodded.

"The boss guessed right the very first time," he paraphrased cheerfully. "You bet I'll be head in name only. Young Ferrers, there's just the man for the job. What d'you say, Archie?"

The latter tried to collect himself. "Of course I accept it, Mr. Fields, and I —I don't think you'll ever regret it." He actually stammered. Was there ever such wonderful luck?

"Oh, that's all right," Mr. Fields went on, "you wouldn't be getting this chance if you didn't deserve it. See here, what about your boarding out at Chestnut Hill for a year or two? Then I can lay my hands on you any time, and you can get hold of things that much sooner. You live on Green Street, don't you? Well, give your landlady a month's notice and quit the 1st of December. A young man coming on like you ought to be thinking of a home anyway. Can't find some nice girl to marry you, what?"

Archie, flushing a little, acknowledged his engagement.

"Good, that's fine!" Then with sudden recollection—" Oh, so you're reformed. Well, I thought you'd get over that. Can't settle down too soon. A lot of nice little cottages out there at Chestnut Hill. Peter, your mother says she wishes you'd come out to dinner to-night. The youngest Wilton girl is to be there, I believe. Guess that's all for this afternoon, Ferrers."

VI.

Archie walked up Chestnut Street on air. "It's better to be born lucky than rich," he reflected. "But I'll be rich, too—and what a lot I can do for Emmy. Glad I didn't tell Mr. Fields now. Wonder what those 'little cottages' out to Chestnut Hill sell for. Emmy—" He stopped short, struck by a sudden realization.

"Why, I must be stark, staring crazy," he said to himself, standing still right in the middle of Chestnut Street. A stout gentleman whom his sudden stopping had seriously incommoded gave him, as he passed by, a vicious prod with his elbow. It started him on again.

"If I hadn't clean forgotten all about it. Oh, Lord, what am I to do? Of course Emmy can't go out to Chestnut Hill to live—well, that would be a give-away. And he advised me to live out there for a year or two—and he knows I'm engaged, and—now—making more than enough to marry on."

He turned aimlessly down 19th Street, and spying Rittenhouse Square sat down in it. The cutting November wind swirled brown, crackling leaves right into his face, but he never saw one of them.

When he arose again, long after his dinner hour, he had made his decision. After all Emmy was a sensible girl; she knew he had only his salary to depend on. And, of course, he wouldn't have to stay out in Chestnut Hill forever. They could buy, or perhaps—he smiled proudly—even build now, far out in West Philadelphia, as far as possible away from Mr. Fields. He'd just ask her to postpone their marriage—perhaps for two years. He sighed a little, for he was very much in love.

"It seems funny that prosperity should make a fellow put off his happiness," he thought ruefully, swinging himself aboard a North 19th Street car.

He decided to go to Plainville and tell her about it—he could go up Saturday afternoon. "Let's see, I can get an express to Harrisburg, and a sleeper to Plainville, and come back Sunday afternoon. Emmy'll like a surprise like that." He thought of their improvised trip to the Academy and how she had made him buy gallery seats. "Lucky she has that little saving streak in her. She'll see through the whole thing like a brick." His simile made him smile. As soon as he reached home he scribbled her a note:

"I'm coming Sunday," he said briefly, "and I have something awfully important to ask you. I'll be there only from 3 to 7. 'When Time let's slip one little perfect hour,' that's that Omar thing you're always quoting, isn't it? Well, there'll be four perfect hours this trip."

All the way on the slow poky local from Harrisburg he pictured her surprise, "I guess she won't mind the postponement one bit," he thought with a brief pang. "She never was keen on marrying. Girls certainly are funny. Here she admits she's in love and willing to marry, and yet she's always hung fire about the date." He dozed fitfully.

As a matter of fact Emmy had fixed the date. "Of course," she said to herself happily, "the 'something important' is that he wants me to marry him right away. Well, I'll tell him that I will, Christmas. Dear old Archie coming all this distance to ask me that. I'll let him beg me two or three times first, and then I'll tell him. Won't he be pleased? I shouldn't be a bit surprised if he went down on his knees again." She, flushed a little, thinking of that first wonderful time.

"Being in love is just—dandy," she decided. "I guess I'll wear my red dress."

Afterward the sight of that red dress always caused Emmy a pang of actual physical anguish. She never saw it without seeing, too, every detail of that disastrous Sunday afternoon. Archie had come—she had gone to the door to meet him—they had lingered happily in the hall a few moments, and then she had brought him in to her mother and Céleste.

The old French woman had kissed him on both cheeks. "See, then it's thou, my cherished one!" she cried ecstatically. "How long a time it is since thou art here."

Mrs. Carrel's greeting, though not so demonstrative, was no less sincere, and when the two were left to themselves "the cherished one" was radiant.

"My, but your mother can make a fellow feel welcome, Emmy. She doesn't say much but what she does, goes."

Emmy smiled a little absently. The gray mist outside in the sombre garden, the fire crackling on the hearth and casting ruddy shadows on Archie's hair, the very red of her dress, Archie himself—all this was making for her a picture, which she saw repeated on endless future Sunday afternoons in Philadelphia. She sighed contentedly.

"I've got something to tell you, sweetheart," said Archie.

"It's coming," she thought. "Oh, isn't it lovely! Of all the people in the world—he loves me, loves me!" She almost missed the beginning of his story. For he was telling her of Mr. Fields and his wonderful offer.

When she finally caught the drift of what he was saying she was vaguely disappointed. He was talking business, in which she was really very little interested. The "saving streak" which Archie had attributed to her was merely sporadic, and was due to a nice girl's delicacy at having money spent on her by a man. But, of course, she listened.

"So you see the future is practically settled—there's only one immediate drawback," he said earnestly. She shut her eyes—it was coming after all.

He went on a little puzzled by her silence; "only one drawback, and that is that, of course, we can't be married for at least two years yet."

Her eyes flew open. "Not marry for two years! Why—why ever not?"

Even then he might have saved the situation by telling her first of his own cruel disappointment, for her loveliness, as she sat there, all glowing red and bronze in the firelit dusk, smote him very strongly.

But he only floundered on.

"Why, Emmy, of course, you can see—you're so much darker than I—anybody can tell at a glance what you—er—are." He was crude, he knew it, but he couldn't see how to help himself. "And we'd have to live at Chestnut Hill, at first, right there near the Fields', and there'd be no way with you there to keep people from knowing that I—that—oh, confound it all—Emmy, you must understand! You don't mind, do you? You know you never were keen on marrying anyway. If we were both the same color—why, Emmy, what is it?"

For she had risen and was looking at him as though he were someone entirely strange. Then she turned and gazed unseeingly out the window. So that was it—the "something important"—he was ashamed of her, of her color; he was always talking about a white man's chances. Why, of course, how foolish she'd been all along—how could he be white with her at his side? And she had thought he had come to urge her to marry him at once—the sting of it sent her head up higher. She turned and faced him, her beautiful silhouette distinctly outlined against the gray blur of the window. She wanted to hurt him—she was quite cool now.

"I have something to tell you, too, Archie," she said evenly. "I've been meaning to tell you for some time. It seems I've been making a mistake all along. I don't really love you"—she was surprised dully that the words didn't choke her—"so, of course, I can't marry you. I was wondering how I could get out of it—you can't think how tiresome it's all been." She had to stop.

He was standing, frozen, motionless like something carved.

"This seems as good an opportunity as any—oh, here's your ring," she finished, holding it out to him coldly. It was a beautiful diamond, small but flawless—the only thing he'd ever gone into debt for.

The statue came to life. "Emmy, you're crazy," he cried passionately, seizing her by the wrist. "You've got the wrong idea. You think I don't want you to marry me. What a cad you must take me for. I only asked you to postpone it a little while, so we'd be happier afterward. I'm doing it all for you, girl. I never dreamed—it's preposterous, Emmy! And you can't say you don't love me—that's all nonsense!"

But she clung to her lie desperately.

"No, really, Archie, I don't love you one bit; of course I like you awfully—let go my wrist, you can think how strong you are. I should have told you long ago, but I hadn't the heart—and it really was interesting." No grand lady on the stage could have been more detached. He should know, too, how it felt not to be wanted.

He was at her feet now, clutching desperately, as she retreated, at her dress—the red dress she had donned so bravely. He couldn't believe in her heartlessness. "You must love me, Emmy, and even if you don't you must marry me anyway. Why, you promised—you don't know what it means to me, Emmy—it's my very life—I've never even dreamed of another woman but you! Take it back, Emmy, you can't mean it."

But she convinced him that she could. "I wish you'd stop, Archie," she said wearily; "this is awfully tiresome. And, anyway, I think you'd better go now if you want to catch your train."

He stumbled to his feet, the life all out of him. In the hall he turned around: "You'll say good-by to your mother for me," he said mechanically. She nodded. He opened the front door. It seemed to close of its own accord behind him.

She came back into the sitting room, wondering why the place had suddenly grown so intolerably hot. She opened a window. From somewhere out of the gray mists came the strains of "Alice, Where Art Thou?" executed with exceeding mournfulness on an organ. The girl listened with a curious detached intentness.

"That must be Willie Holborn," she thought; "no one else could play as wretchedly as that." She crossed heavily to the armchair and flung herself in it. Her mind seemed to go on acting as though it were clockwork and she were watching it.

ONCE SHE SAID: "NOW THIS, I SUPPOSE, IS WHAT THEY CALL A TRAGEDY."

Once she said: "Now this, I suppose, is what they call a tragedy." And again: "He did get down on his knees."

VII.

There was nothing detached or impersonal in Archie's consideration of his plight. All through the trip home, through the long days that followed and the still longer nights, he was in torment. Again and again he went over the scene.

"She was making a plaything out of me," he chafed bitterly. "All these months she's been only fooling. And yet I wonder if she really meant it, if she didn't just do it to make it easier for me to be white. If that's the case what an insufferable cad she must take me for. No, she couldn't have cared for me, because if she had she'd have seen through it all right away."

By the end of ten days he had worked himself almost into a fever. His burning face and shaking hands made him resolve, as he dressed that morning, to 'phone the office that he was too ill to come to work.

"And I'll stay home and write her a letter that she'll have to answer." For although he had sent her one and sometimes two letters every day ever since his return, there had been no reply.

"She must answer that," he said to himself at length, when the late afternoon shadows were creeping in. He had torn up letter after letter—he had been proud and beseeching by turns. But in this last he had laid his very heart bare.

"And if she doesn't answer it"—it seemed to him he couldn't face the possibility. He was at the writing desk where her picture stood in its little silver frame. It had been there all that day. As a rule he kept it locked up, afraid of what it might reveal to his landlady's vigilant eye. He sat there, his head bowed over the picture, wondering dully how he should endure his misery.

Someone touched him on the shoulder.

"Gad, boy," said Mr. Nicholas Fields, "here I thought you were sick in bed, and come here to find you mooning over a picture. What's the matter? Won't the lady have you? Let's see who it is that's been breaking you up so." Archie watched him in fascinated horror, while he picked up the photograph and walked over to the window. As he scanned it his expression changed.

"Oh," he said, with a little puzzled frown and yet laughing, too, "it's your colored lady friend again. Won't she let you go? That's the way with these black women, once they get hold of a white man—bleed 'em to death. I don't see how you can stand them anyway; it's the Spanish in you, I suppose. Better get rid of her before you get married. Hello—" he broke off.

For Archie was standing menacingly over him. "If you say another word about that girl I'll break every rotten bone in your body."

"Oh, come," said Mr. Fields, still pleasant, "isn't that going it a little too strong? Why, what can a woman like that mean to you?"

"She can mean," said the other slowly, "everything that the woman who has promised to be my wife ought to mean." The broken engagement meant nothing in a time like this.

Mr. Fields forgot his composure. "To be your wife! Why, you idiot, you—you'd ruin yourself—marry a Negro—have you lost your senses? Oh, I suppose it's some of your crazy foreign notions. In this country white gentlemen don't marry colored women."

Archie had not expected this loophole. He hesitated, then with a shrug he burnt all his bridges behind him. One by one he saw his ambitions flare up and vanish.

"No, you're right," he rejoined. "White gentlemen don't, but colored men do." Then he waited calmly for the avalanche.

It came. "You mean," said Mr. Nicholas Fields, at first with only wonder and then with growing suspicion in his voice, "you mean that you're colored?" Archie nodded and watched him turn into a maniac.

"Why, you low-lived young blackguard, You—" he swore horribly. "And you've let me think all this time—" He broke off again, hunting for something insulting enough to say. "You Nigger!" he hurled at him. He really felt there was nothing worse, so he repeated it again and again with fresh imprecations.

"I think," said Archie, "that that will do. I shouldn't like to forget myself, and I'm in a pretty reckless mood to-day. You must remember, Mr. Fields, you didn't ask me who I was, and I had no occasion to tell you. Of course I won't come back to the office."

"If you do," said Mr. Fields, white to the lips, "I'll have you locked up if I have to perjure my soul to find a charge against you. I'll show you what a white man can do—you—"

But Archie had taken him by the shoulder and pushed him outside the door.

"And that's all right," he said to himself with a sudden heady sense of liberty. He surveyed himself curiously in the mirror. "Wouldn't anybody think I had changed into some horrible ravening beast. Lord, how that one little word changed him." He ruminated over the injustice—the petty, foolish injustice of the whole thing.

"I don't believe," he said slowly, "it's worth while having a white man's chances if one has to be like that. I see what Emmy used to be driving at now." The thought of her sobered him.

"If it should be on account of my chances that you're letting me go," he assured the picture gravely, "it's all quite unnecessary, for I'll never have another opportunity like that."

In which he was quite right. It even looked as though he couldn't get any work at all along his own line. There was no demand for colored engineers.

"If you keep your mouth shut," one man said, "and not let the other clerks know what you are I might try you for awhile." There was nothing for him to do but accept. At the end of two weeks—the day before Thanksgiving—he found out that the men beside him, doing exactly the same kind of work as his own, were receiving for it five dollars more a week. The old injustice based on color had begun to hedge him in. It seemed to him that his unhappiness and humiliation were more than he could stand.

VIII.

But at least his life was occupied. Emmy, on the other hand, saw her own life stretching out through endless vistas of empty, useless days. She grew thin and listless, all the brightness and vividness of living toned down for her into one gray, flat monotony. By Thanksgiving Day the strain showed its effects on her very plainly.

Her mother, who had listened in her usual silence when her daughter told her the cause of the broken engagement, tried to help her.

"Emmy," she said, "you're probably doing Archie an injustice. I don't believe he ever dreamed of being ashamed of you. I think it is your own wilful pride that is at fault. You'd better consider carefully—if you are making a mistake you'll regret it to the day of your death. The sorrow of it will never leave you."

Emmy was petulant. "Oh, mother, what can you know about it? Céleste says you married when you were young, even younger than I—married to the man you loved, and you were with him, I suppose, till he died. You couldn't know how I feel." She fell to staring absently out the window. It was a long time before her mother spoke again.

"No, Emmy," she finally began again very gravely, "I wasn't with your father till he died. That is why I'm speaking to you as I am. I had sent him away—we had quarrelled—oh, I was passionate enough when I was your age, Emmy. He was jealous—he was a West Indian—I suppose Céleste has told you—and one day he came past the sitting room—it was just like this one, overlooking the garden. Well, as he glanced in the window he saw a man, a white man, put his arms around me and kiss me. When he came in through the side door the man had gone. I was just about to explain—no, tell him—for I didn't know he had seen me when he began." She paused a little, but presently went on in her even, dispassionate voice:

"He was furious, Emmy; oh, he was so angry, and he accused me—oh, my dear! He was almost insane. But it was really because he loved me. And then I became angry and I wouldn't tell him anything. And finally, Emmy, he struck me—you mustn't blame him, child; remember, it was the same spirit showing in both of us, in different ways. I was doing all I could to provoke him by keeping silence and he merely retaliated in his way. The blow wouldn't have harmed a little bird. But—well, Emmy, I think I must have gone crazy. I ordered him from the house—it had been my mother's—and I told him never, never to let me see him again." She smiled drearily.

"I never did see him again. After he left Céleste and I packed up our things and came here to America. You were the littlest thing, Emmy. You can't remember living in France at all, can you? Well, when your father found out where I was he wrote and asked me to forgive him and to let him come back. 'I am on my knees,' the letter said. I wrote and told him yes—I loved him, Emmy; oh, child, you with your talk of color; you don't know what love is. If you really loved Archie you'd let him marry you and lock you off, away from all the world, just so long as you were with him.

"I was so happy," she resumed. "I hadn't seen him for two years. Well, he started—he was in Hayti then; he got to New York safely and started here. There was a wreck—just a little one—only five people killed, but he was one of them. He was so badly mangled, they wouldn't even let me see him."

"Oh!" breathed Emmy. "Oh, mother!" After a long time she ventured a question. "Who was the other man, mother?"

"The other man? Oh! that was my father; my mother's guardian, protector, everything, but not her husband. She was a slave, you know, in New Orleans, and he helped her to get away. He took her to Hayti first, and then, afterward, sent her over to France, where I was born. He never ceased in his kindness. After my mother's death I didn't see him for ten years, not till after I was married. That was the time Emile—you were named for your father, you know—saw him kiss me. Mr. Pechegru, my father, was genuinely attached to my mother, I think, and had come after all these years to make some reparation. It was through him I first began translating for the publishers. You know yourself how my work has grown."

She was quite ordinary and matter of fact again. Suddenly her manner changed. "I lost him when I was 22. Emmy—think of it—and my life has been nothing ever since. That's why I want you to think—to, consider—" She was weeping passionately now.

Her mother in tears! To Emmy it was as though the world lay in ruins about her feet.

IX.

As it happened Mrs. Carrel's story only plunged her daughter into deeper gloom.

"It couldn't have happened at all if we hadn't been colored," she told herself moodily. "If grandmother hadn't been colored she wouldn't have been a slave, and if she hadn't been a slave—That's what it is, color—color—it's wrecked mother's life and now it's wrecking mine."

She couldn't get away from the thought of it. Archie's words, said so long ago, came back to her: "Just wait till color keeps you from the thing you want the most," he had told her.

"It must be wonderful to be white," she said to herself, staring absently at the Stevenson motto on the wall of her little room. She went up close and surveyed it unseeingly. "If only I weren't colored," she thought. She checked herself angrily, enveloped by a sudden sense of shame. "It doesn't seem as though I could be the same girl."

A thin ray of cold December sunlight picked out from the motto a little gilded phrase: "To renounce when that shall be necessary and not be embittered." She read it over and over and smiled whimsically.

"I've renounced—there's no question about that," she thought, "but no one could expect me not to be bitter."

If she could just get up strength enough, she reflected, as the days passed by, she would try to be cheerful in her mother's presence. But it was so easy to be melancholy.

About a week before Christmas her mother went to New York. She would see her publishers and do some shopping and would be back Christmas Eve. Emmy was really glad to see her go.

"I'll spend that time in getting myself together," she told herself, "and when mother comes back I'll be all right." Nevertheless, for the first few days she was, if anything, more listless than ever. But Christmas Eve and the prospect of her mother's return gave her a sudden brace.

"Without bitterness," she kept saying to herself, "to renounce without bitterness." Well, she would—she would. When her mother came back she should be astonished. She would even wear the red dress. But the sight of it made her weak; she couldn't put it on. But she did dress herself very carefully in white, remembering how gay she had been last Christmas Eve. She had put mistletoe in her hair and Archie had taken it out.

"I don't have to have mistletoe," he had whispered to her proudly.

In the late afternoon she ran out to Holborn's. As she came back 'round the corner she saw the stage drive away. Her mother, of course, had come. She ran into the sitting room wondering why the door was closed.

"I will be all right," she said to herself, her hand on the knob, and stepped into the room—to walk straight into Archie's arms.

She clung to him as though she could never let him go.

"Oh, Archie, you've come back, you really wanted me."

He strained her closer. "I've never stopped wanting you," he told her, his lips on her hair.

Presently, when they were sitting by the fire, she in the armchair and he at her feet, he began to explain. She would not listen at first, it was all her fault, she said.

"No, indeed," he protested generously, "it was mine. I was so crude; it's a wonder you can care at all about anyone as stupid as I am. And I think I was too ambitious—though in a way it was all for you, Emmy; you must always believe that. But I'm at the bottom rung now, sweetheart; you see, I told Mr. Fields everything and—he put me out."

"Oh, Archie," she praised him, "that was really noble, since you weren't obliged to tell him."

"Well, but in one sense I was obliged to—to keep my self-respect, you know. So there wasn't anything very noble about it after all." He couldn't tell her what had really happened. "I'm genuinely poor now, dearest, but your mother sent for me to come over to New York. She knows some pretty all-right people there—she's a wonderful woman, Emmy—and I'm to go out to the Philippines. Could you—do you think you could come out there, Emmy?"

She could, she assured him, go anywhere. "Only don't let it be too long, Archie—I—"

He was ecstatic. "Emmy—you—you don't mean you would be willing to start out there with me, do you? Why, that's only three months off. When —" He stopped, peering out the window. "Who is that coming up the path?"

"It's Willie Holborn," said Emmy. "I suppose Mary sent him around with my present. Wait, I'll let him in."

But it wasn't Willie Holborn, unless he had been suddenly converted into a small and very grubby special-delivery boy.

"Mr. A. Ferrers," he said laconically, thrusting a book out at her. "Sign here."

She took the letter back into the pleasant room, and A. Ferrers, scanning the postmark, tore it open. "It's from my landlady; she's the only person in Philadelphia who knows where I am. Wonder what's up?" he said incuriously. "I know I didn't forget to pay her my bill. Hello, what's this?" For within was a yellow envelope—a telegram.

Together they tore it open.

"Don't be a blooming idiot," it read; "the governor says come back and receive apologies and accept job. Merry Christmas.

"PETER FIELDS."

"Oh," said Emmy, "isn't it lovely? Why does he say 'receive apologies,' Archie?"

"Oh, I don't know," he quibbled, reflecting that if Peter hadn't said just that his return would have been as impossible as ever. "It's just his queer way of talking. He's the funniest chap! Looks as though I wouldn't have to go to the Philippines after all. But that doesn't alter the main question. How soon do you think you can marry me, Emmy?"

His voice was light, but his eyes—

"Well," said Emmy bravely, "what do you think of Christmas?"

MY HOUSE AND A GLIMPSE OF MY LIFE THEREIN

Far away on the top of a gently sloping hill stands my house. On one side the hill slopes down into a valley, the site of a large country town; on the other it descends into a forest, thick with lofty trees and green, growing things. Here in stately solitude amid such surroundings towers my dwelling; its dull-red brick is barely visible through the thick ivy, but the gleaming tops of its irregular roof and sloping gables catch the day's sunlight and crown it with a crown of gold.

An irregular, rambling building is this house of mine, built on no particular plan, following no order save that of desire and fancy. Peculiarly jutting rooms appear, and unsuspected towers and bay-windows,—the house seems almost to have built itself and to have followed its own will in so doing. If there be any one distinct feature at all, it is that halls long and very broad traverse the various parts of the house, separating a special set of rooms here, making another division there. Splendid halls are these, with fire-places and cosy arm-chairs, and delightful, dark corners, and mysterious closets, and broad, shallow stairs. Just the place in winter for a host of young people to gather before the fire-place, and with pop-corn and chestnuts, stories and apples, laugh away the speeding hours, while the wind howls without.

The hall on the ground floor has smaller corridors that branch off and lead at their extremity into the garden. Surely, no parterre of the East, perfumed with the odors of Araby, and peopled with houris, was ever so fair as my garden! Surely, nowhere does the snow lie so pure and smooth and deep, nowhere are the evergreen trees so very tall and stately as in my garden in winter! Most glorious is it in late spring and early June. Out on the green, green sward I sit under the blossoming trees; in sheer delightful idleness I spend my hours, listening to the blending of wind-song with the "sweet jargoning" of little birds. If a shower threatens I flee across my garden's vast expanse, past the gorgeous rosebushes and purple lilacs, and safe within my little summer-house, watch the "straight-falling rain," and think of other days, and sighing wish that Kathleen and I had not parted in anger that far-off morning.

When the shower ceases, I hasten down the broad path, under the shelter of lofty trees, until I reach one of my house's many doors. Once within, but still in idle mood, I perch myself on a window-seat and look toward the town. Tall spires and godly church steeples rise before me; high above all climbs the town clock; farther over in the west, smoke is curling from the foundries. How busy is the life beyond my house! Through the length of the long hall to the window at the opposite side I go, and watch the friendly nodding of tall trees and the tender intercourse of all this beautiful green life. Suddenly the place becomes transformed—this is an enchanted forest, the Forest Morgraunt—in and out among the trees pass valiant knights and distressed ladies. Prosper le Gai rides to the rescue of Isoult la Desirous. Surely, the forest life beyond my house is full of purpose and animation, too.

From the window I roam past the sweet, familiar chambers, to the attic staircase, with its half-hidden angles and crazy old baluster. Up to the top of the house I go, to a dark little storeroom under the eaves. I open the trap-door in the middle of the ceiling, haul down a small ladder, mount its deliciously wobbly length, and behold, I am in my chosen domain—a queen come into her very own! If I choose I can convert it into a dread and inaccessible fortress, by drawing up my ladder and showering nutshells and acorns down on the heads of would-be intruders. Safe from all possible invasion, I browse through the store of old, old magazines and quaint books and journals, or wander half-timidly through my infinite unexplored land of mystery, picking my way past heaps of delightful rubbish and strong, secret chests, fancying goblins in the shadowy corners, or watching from the little windows the sunbeams' play on the garden, and the grey-blue mist hanging far-off over the hollow valley.

From such sights and fancies I descend to my library, there to supplement my flitting ideas with the fixed conception of others. Although I love every brick and little bit of mortar in my dwelling, my library is of all portions the very dearest to me. In this part of the house more than any place else, have those irregular rooms been added, to receive my ever-increasing store of books. In the large room,—the library proper—is a broad, old-fashioned fire-place, and on the rug in front I lie and read, and read again, all the dear simple tales of earlier days, "Mother Goose," "Alice in Wonderland," "The Arabian Nights"; here, too, I revel in modern stories of impossible adventure. But when a storm rises at night, say, and the rain beats and dashes, and all without is raging, I draw a huge, red arm-chair before the fire and curl into its hospitable depths.

> "And there I sit
> Reading old things,
> Of knights and lorn damsels,
> While the wind sings—
> Oh, drearily sings!"*

Off in one of the little side-rooms stands my desk, covered with books that have caught my special fancy and awakened my thoughts. This is my *living*-room, where I spend my moods of bitterness and misunderstanding, and questioning, and joy, too, I think. Often in the midst of a heap of books, the Rubaiyat and a Bible, Walter Pater's Essays and "Robert Elsmere" and "Aurora Leigh," and books of belief, of insinuation, of open unbelief, I bow my head on my desk in a passion of doubt

---

* A stanza from the poem "Old Song" by Edward Fitzgerald.

and ignorance and longing, and ponder, ponder. Here on this desk is a book in which I jot down all the little, beautiful word-wonders, whose meanings are so often unknown to me, but whose very mystery I love. I write, "In Vishnu Land what Avatar?" and "After the red pottage comes the exceedingly bitter cry," and all the other sweet, incomprehensible fragments that haunt my memory so.

High up on many of the shelves in the many rooms are books as yet unread by me, Schopenhauer and Gorky, Petrarch and Sappho, Goethe and Kant and Schelling; much of Ibsen, Plato and Ennius and Firdausi, and Lafcadis Hearn,—a few of these in the original. With such reading in store for me, is not my future rich?

Can such a house as this one of mine be without immediate and vivid impression on its possessor? First and most of all it imbues me with a strong sense of home; banishment from my house would surely be life's most bitter sorrow. It is so eminently and fixedly mine, my very own, that the mere possession of it,—a house not yours or another's, but mine, to live in as I will,—is very sweet to me. It is absolutely the *chez soi* of my soul's desire. With this sense of ownership, a sense which is deeper than I can express, a sense which is almost a longing for some unknown, unexplainable, entire possession—passionate, spiritual absorption of my dwelling—comes a feeling that is almost terror. Is it right to feel thus, to have this vivid, permeating and yet wholly intellectual enjoyment of the material loveliness and attractiveness of my house? May this not be perhaps a sensuality of the mind, whose influence may be more insidious, more pernicious, more powerful to unfit me for the real duties of life than are other lower and yet more open forms of enjoyment? Oh, I pray not! My house is inexpressibly dear to me, but the light of the ideal beyond, "the light that never was on sea or land," is dearer still.

This, then, is my house, and this, in measure, is my life in my house. Here, amid my favorite books, and pictures, and fancies, and longings, and sweet mysteries, shall old age come upon me, in fashion most inglorious, but in equal degree most peaceful and happy. *Perhaps*—that is! For after all my house is constructed of dream-fabric, and the place of its building is—*Spain!*

THERE WAS ONE TIME!

ANNA.

"There was one time" began the freckled-faced boy. Miss Fetter interrupted him with emphasis—"but that is not idiomatic, our expression for *il y avait une fois* is 'once upon a time.' The value of a translation lies in its adequacy." And for the fiftieth time that term she launched into an explanation of the translation of idioms. The class listened with genial composure—the more she talked, the less they could read. She reached her peroration. "Do you understand, Master Reynolds?"

The freckled-faced boy, who had been surreptitiously consulting his vocabulary, turned deftly back to the passage. "Yes'm," he nodded. "There was one time"—he began again unabashed.

Miss Fetter sighed and passed on to another pupil. Between them all there was evolved in hopelessly unsympathetic English the story of a dainty French shepherdess who growing tired of her placid sheep left them to shift for themselves one gorgeous spring-day, donned her sky-blue dress, traversed the sombre forest and came to another country. There she met the prince who, struck with her charm and naiveté, asked her to play with him. So she did until sunset when he escorted her to the edge of the forest where she pursued her way home to her little thatched cottage, with a mind much refreshed and "garlanded with pleasant memories."

The pupils read, as pupils will, with stolid indifference. The fairy-tale was merely so many pages of French to them, as indeed it was to Miss Fetter. That she must teach foreign languages—always her special detestation—seemed to her the final irony of an ironic existence.

"It's all so inadequate," she fumed to herself, pinning on her hat before the tiny mirror in the little stuffy teachers' room. She was old enough to have learned very thoroughly all the aphorisms of her day. She believed that all service performed honestly and thoroughly was helpful, but she was still too young to know that such was literally true and her helplessness irked her. See her, then, as she walked home through the ugly streets of Marytown, neither white nor black, of medium height, slim, nose neither good nor bad, mouth beautiful, teeth slightly irregular, but perfect. Altogether, when she graduated at eighteen from the Business High School in Philadelphia she was as much as any one else the typical American girl done over in brown, no fears for the future, no regrets for the past, rather glad to put her schoolbooks down for good and decidedly glad that she was no longer to be a burden on her parents.

Getting a position after all was not so easy. Perhaps for the first time she began to realize the handicap of color. Her grade on graduation had been "meritorious." She had not shone, but neither had she been stupid.

She had rarely volunteered to answer questions, being mostly occupied in dreaming, but she could answer when called on. If she had no self-assurance, neither had she a tendency to self-belittlement. Her English, if not remarkable, was at least correct; her typewriting was really irreproachable; her spelling exact; and she had the quota of useless French —or German—vocabulary which the average pupil brings out of the average High School. Perhaps it was because she had lived all her life in a small up-town street in a white neighborhood and played with most of the boys and girls there, perhaps it was because at eighteen one is still idealistic that she answered advertisement after advertisement without apprehension. The result, of course, was always the same; always the faint shock of surprise in the would-be employer's voice, the faint stare, the faint emphasis—"You! Oh no, the position is not open to—er—you." At first she did not understand, but even when she did she kept futilely on—she could not, she would not teach—and why does one graduate from a Business High School, if one is not to be employed by a business firm?

That summer her father, a silent, black man, died and her decisions against teaching fled. She was not a normal school graduate, so she could not teach in Philadelphia. The young German drummer next door told her of positions to be had in colored schools in the South—perhaps she could teach her favorite stenography or drawing in which she really excelled. Fate at that point took on her most menacing aspect. Nothing that was not menial came her way, excepting work along lines of which she knew nothing. Her mother and she gave up the little house and the two of them went to service. Those two awful years gave Anna her first real taste of the merciless indifference of life. Her mother, a woman of nerveless and, to Anna, enviable stolidity found, as always, a refuge in inapt quotations of Scripture. But Anna lived in a fever of revolt. She spent her days as a waitress and her evenings in night school trying feverishly to learn some of those subjects which she might have taught, had she been properly prepared. At the end of two years the change came carelessly, serenely, just as though it might always have happened. The son-in-law of Mrs. Walton, for whom she worked, passed through town late one night. The family had gone out and for want of something better he had, as he ate his solitary dinner, asked the rather taciturn waitress about her history. She had told him briefly and he had promised her, with equal brevity, a position as drawing teacher in a colored seminary of which he was a trustee. Anna, stunned, went with her mother to Maryville. Just as suddenly as it started, the struggle for existence was over, though, of course, they were still poor. Mrs. Fetter found plenty of plain sewing to do and Anna was appointed. But Fate, with a last malevolence, saw to it that she was appointed to teach History and French, which were just being introduced into the seminary. She thought of this as she opened her mother's gate,—the irony of the thing made her sick. "Since my luck was going to change, why couldn't I have been allowed to teach mechanical drawing," she wondered, "or given a chance at social work? But teaching French! I suppose the reason that little shepherdess neglected her sheep that day was because *they* were French."

II

Still one cannot persist in gloom when it is April and one is twenty-six and looks, as only American girls, whether white or brown, can look, five years younger. Anna, hastening down the street in her best blue serge dress, her pretty slim feet in faultless tan shoes, felt her moodiness, which had almost become habitual, vanish.

The wearing of the blue dress was accidental. She had come down to breakfast in her usual well-worn gray skirt and immaculate shirt-waist in time to hear her small cousin, Theophilus, proclaim his latest enterprise. A boy was going to give him five white mice for his pen-knife and he was going to bring them home right after school and put them in a little cage. Pretty soon there'd be more of them—"they have lots of children, Aunt Emmeline, and I'm going to sell them and buy Sidney Williams' ukulele, and"—

"Indeed you are going to do no such thing," exclaimed Anna, her high good humor vanishing. "Mother, you won't let him bring those nasty things here, I know. As for keeping them in a cage, they'd be all over the house in no time."

But Mrs. Fetter, who loved Theophilus because he was still a little boy and she could baby him, opined that foxes and birds had their nests. "Let's see the cage, Philly dear, maybe they can't get out."

The rest had followed as the night the day. Theophilus, rushing from the table, had knocked Anna's cup of cocoa out of her hand and the brown liquid had run down the front of the immaculate blouse and settled in a comfortable pool in her lap.

"Oh well," her mother had said, unmoved as usual, "run along, Anna, and put on your blue serge dress. It won't do you any harm to wear it this once and if you hurry you'll get to school in time just the same. You didn't go to do it, did you, Philly?"

Theophilus, aghast, had fled to the shelter of his banjo from which he was extracting plaintive strains. He played banjo, guitar and piano with equal and indeed amazing facility, but as his musical tastes were surprisingly eclectic, the results were at times distressing. Anna, hastening out, a real vision now in her pretty frock, an unwonted color in her smooth bronze cheeks, heard him telling his aunt again about the ukulele which Sidney Williams owned but couldn't play. "It's broke. Some folks where his father works gave it to him. Betcher I'll fix it and play it, too, when I get hold of it," his high voice was proclaiming confidently.

"I suppose he will,"—thought his cousin, "I hope that North street car won't be hung up this morning. He ought to make a fine musician, but, of course, he won't get a chance at it when he grows up." The memory of her own ironic calling stung her. "He'll probably have to be a farmer just because he'll hate it. I do wish I could walk, it's so lovely. I wish I were that little shepherdess off on a holiday. She was wearing a blue dress, I remember."

Well, her mind leaped up to the thought. Why shouldn't she take a day off? In all these six years she had never been out once, except the time Theophilus had had the measles. The street car came up at this point, waited an infinitesimal second and clanged angrily off, as if provoked at its own politeness. She looked after it with mingled dismay and amusement. "I'd be late anyway," she told herself, "now that I've lost that car. I'll get a magazine and explore the Park; no one will know."

Two hours of leisurely strolling brought her to Hertheimer Park, a small green enclosure at the end of the ugly little town. Anna picked her way past groups of nursemaids and idlers looking in newspapers for occupation which they hoped they would never find. She came at last to the little grove in the far side of the Park where the sun was not quite so high and, seating herself near the fountain, began to feed the squirrels with some of the crackers which she had bought in one of the corner groceries.

Being alive was pretty decent after all, she reflected. Life was the main thing—teaching school, being colored, even being poor were only aspects, her mind went on. If one were just well and comfortable—not even rich or pampered—one could get along; the thing to do was to look at life in the large and not to gaze too closely at the specific interest or activity in hand. Her growing philosophy tickled her sense of humor. "You didn't feel like that when you were at Mrs. Walton's," she told herself bluntly and smiled at her own discomfiture.

"That's right, smile at me," said an oily voice, and she looked up to see one of the idlers leaning over the back of her bench. "You're a right good lookin' gal. How'd you like to take a walk with me?"

She stared into his evil face, fascinated. Where, where, where were all the people? The nurse-maids had vanished, the readers of newspapers had gone—to buy afternoon editions, perhaps. She felt herself growing icy, paralyzed. "You needn't think I mind your being a nigger," went on the hateful voice, "I ruther like 'em. I hain't what you might call prejudiced."

This was what could happen to you if you were a colored girl who felt like playing at being a French shepherdess. She looked around for help and exactly as though at a cue in a play, as though he had been waiting for that look a young colored man stepped forward, one hand courteously lifting his hat, the other resting carelessly in his hip-pocket. "Good afternoon, Miss Walker," he said, and his whole bearing exhaled courtesy. "I couldn't be sure it was you until you turned around. I'm sorry I'm late, I hope I haven't kept you waiting. I hope you weren't annoying my friend," he addressed the tramp pleasantly.

But the latter, with one fascinated glance at that hand still immobile in that suggestive hip-pocket, was turning away.

"I was jus askin' a direction," he muttered. "I'll be going now."

III

The two young colored people stared at each other in silence. Anna spoke first—

"Of course, my name isn't Walker," she murmured inadequately.

They both laughed at that, she nervously and he weakly. The uncertain quality of his laughter made her eye him sharply. "Why, you're trembling —all over," she exclaimed, and then with the faintest curl of her lip, "you'd better sit down if you're as much afraid as all that," her mind ended.

He did sit down, still with that noticeable deference, and, removing his hat, mopped his forehead. His hair was black and curly above a very pleasant brown face, she noted subconsciously, but her conscious self was saying "He was afraid, because he's colored."

He seemed to read her thoughts. "I guess you think I'm a fine rescuer," he smiled at her ruefully. "You see, I'm just beginning to recover from an attack of malarial fever. That is why I pretended to have a gun. I'm afraid I couldn't have tackled him successfully, this plagued fever always leaves me so weak, but I'd have held him off till you had got away. I didn't want him to touch you, you seemed so nice and dainty. I'd been watching you for sometime under the trees, thinking how very American you were and all that sort of thing, and when you smiled it seemed to me such a bit of all right that you should be feeling so fit and self-confident. When I saw the expression on your face change I almost wept to think I hadn't the strength to bash his head in. That was why I waited to catch your eye, because I didn't want to startle you and I didn't have strength for anything but diplomacy."

She nodded, ashamed of her unkindness and interested already in something else. "Aren't you foreign?" she ventured, "You seem different somehow, something in the way you talk made me feel perhaps you weren't American."

"Well I am," he informed her heartily. "I was born, of all places, in Camden, New Jersey, and if that doesn't make me American I don't know what does. But I've been away a long time, I must admit, that's why my accent sounds a little odd, I suppose. My father went to British Guiana when I was ten; but I got the idea that I wanted to see some more foreign countries, so when I was fifteen I ran away to England. You couldn't imagine, a girl like you, all the things I've seen and done, and the kinds of people I've known. I had such an insatiable thirst for adventure, a sort of compelling curiosity."

He paused, plainly reminiscent.

"I've picked up all sorts of trades in England and France—I love France and it was my stay there that made me long so much to get back to America. I kept the idea before me for years. It seemed to me that to live under a republican form of government, with lots of my own people around me, would be the finest existence in the world. I remember I used to tell a crowd of American chaps I was working with in France about it, and they used to be so amused and seemed to have some sort of secret joke."

Anna thought it highly probable.

He looked at her meditating. "Yes, I suppose they had—from their point of view but not from mine. You see," he told her with an oddly boyish air of bestowing a confidence, "life as life is intensely interesting to me. I wake up every morning—except when I have malarial fever"—he interrupted himself whimsically—"wondering what I'll have to overcome during the day. And it's different things in different environments. In this country it's color, for instance, in another it might be ignorance of the native tongue.

"When I came back to New York I was a little non-plussed, I must confess, at the extraordinary complexes of prejudice. I went to a nice-looking hotel and they didn't want me a bit at first. Well, I pick up the idiom of a language very quickly and I suppose at this point my English accent and expression out-Englished most Englishmen's. After a bit the clerk asked where I hailed from and when I told him Manchester, and displayed my baggage—only I called it luggage—all covered with labels, he said 'oh, that was different,' and gave me a room just as right as you please. Well it struck me so peculiarly idiotic to refuse your own countryman because he is brown, but to take him in, though he hasn't changed a particle, because he hails from another country. But it gave me a clue."

"Yes?" she wondered.

"You see, it made me angry that I had allowed myself to take refuge under my foreign appearance, when what I really wanted to do was to wave my hat and shout, 'I'm an American and I've come home. Aren't you glad to see me? If you only knew how proud I am to be here.' The disappointment and the sting of it kept me awake all night. And next day I went out and met up with some colored fellows—nice chaps all right—and they got me some rooms up in Harlem. Ever see Harlem?" he asked her,—"most interesting place, America done over in color. Well it was just what I wanted after Europe.

"But it struck me there was a lack of self-esteem, a lack of self-appreciation, and a tendency to measure ourselves by false ideals." He was clearly on his hobby now, his deep-set eyes glowed, his wide, pleasant mouth grew firmer.

"Your average British or French man of color and every Eastern man of color thinks no finer creature than himself ever existed. I wanted to tell our folks that there is nothing more supremely American than the colored American, nothing more made-in-America, so to speak. There is no supreme court which rules absolutely that white is the handsomest color, that straight hair is the most alluring. If we could just realize the warmth and background which we supply to America, the mellowness, the rhythm, the music. Heavens," he broke off, "where does one ever hear such music as some of the most ordinary colored people can bring out of a piano?"

Anna, thinking of Theophilus, smiled.

"And there's something else too," he resumed. "The cold-bloodedness which enables a civilized people to maim and kill in the Congo and on the Putumayo, or to lynch in Georgia, isn't in it with the simple kindliness which we find in almost any civilized colored man. No people has a keener, more rollicking humor, and the music—

"Excuse my ranting," he begged, all apology, "but I get so excited about it all. Did you ever read any Pater?" he asked her abruptly.

"No," she told him shamefacedly—Pater was not included in her High School English and she had read almost no literature since.

He nodded indifferently. "Well, in 'The Child in the House,' the chap says if he had his way he wouldn't give very poor people 'the things men desire most, but the power to realize and taste at will a certain desirable, clear light in the new morning.' That's me," he concluded, too earnest to care about grammar. "I'd give us the power to realize how wonderful and beautiful and enduring we are in the world's scheme of things. I can't help but feel that finally a man is taken at his own estimate."

They were silent a moment, watching a flock of pale, yellow butterflies waver like an aura over a bed of deep golden crocuses.

"Have you told your views to many people?" Anna asked him a trifle shyly. His mood, his experiences, his whole personality seemed so remote from anything she had ever encountered.

"No," he told her dryly. "I haven't done anything. I came from New York down to this town to visit my aunt, my mother's youngest sister—she's as young as I am, by the way, isn't that funny? And I've had the malarial fever ever since. I get it every spring, darn it! " He ended in total disgust.

"You might tell me something of yourself. We'll probably never see each other again," he suggested lingeringly, with just the faintest question-mark in his voice.

But Anna didn't catch it, she was too absorbed in the prospect of having some one with whom to discuss her perplexities. She launched out without a thought for the amazing unconventionality of the whole situation. "And so," she finished, "here I am painfully teaching French. I don't make enough to allow me to go to summer school and I don't seem to make much progress by myself." He seemed so terribly competent that she hated to let him know how stupid she was. Still, it was a relief to admit it.

"I know," he comforted her. "You needn't feel so very bad, there are some things that just don't come to one. I'm a mechanical engineer and I can read any kind of plans but it worries me to death to have to draw them."

"Why, I can draw," she told him—"anything."

Their first constraint fell upon them.

He tried to break it. “If you teach,” he asked her, “What are you doing here? Wednesday isn’t a holiday, is it?”

She broke out laughing. “No, it’s too funny! You wouldn’t believe how it all happened”—and she told him the story of the little shepherdess. “And this morning my little cousin spilt cocoa all over my school clothes and I had to put on my blue dress. It made me think of the little shepherdess and here I am.”

He was watching her intently. How charming she was with all that color in her face. Comely, that was the word for her and—wholesome. He was sure of it.

“How did the story end?” he wondered.

She didn’t know, she told him, shamefaced anew at her stupidity. “You know it is so hard for me, every year we read a new book and I never get a chance to get used to the vocabulary. And so the night before I just get the lessons out for the next day. I teach six preparations, you see, three in history and three in French. And it takes me such a long time I never read ahead. I simply cannot get the stuff,” she explained, much downcast.

“I’ve tried awfully hard; but you know some people have absolutely no feeling for a foreign language. I’m one of them! As for composition work”—she shook her head miserably, “I have to dig for it so. The only thing is that I can feel whether a translation is adequate or not, so I don’t mind that part of the work. But when we got that far in this story the head language teacher—crazy thing, she’s always changing about—said to lay that aside and finish up all the grammar and then go back and do all the translating. I’ve never looked at the story since. All I know,” she ended thoughtlessly, “is that the shepherdess played and talked with the prince all day and he took her to the edge of the forest at sunset—what’s the matter?” she broke off.

"UNCLE DICK."

"You didn't tell me," he said a trifle breathless, "that she met a prince."

"Didn't I? Well she did—and it's four o'clock and I must go. My mother will be wondering where I am." She held out her ungloved hand, shapely and sizeable and very comely. It took him some time to shake hands, but perhaps that was one of his foreign ways.

She had gone and he stood staring after her. Then he settled back on the bench again, hat over his eyes, hands in his pockets, long legs stretched out in front of him.

"Of course," he was thinking, "you can't say to a girl like that, 'well, if you're playing shepherdess let me play your prince?' Wasn't she nice, though, so fine and wholesome—and colored. Tommy was playing last night with that What's that thing Tommy was playing last night with that little Theophilus somebody? Oh yes,"—he hummed it melodiously:

"'I'm for you, brown-skin.'"

IV

Not until June did Anna encounter the little shepherdess again.

She settled down the night before the lesson was due to read it with a great deal of interest. Her meeting with "the prince," as she always called the strange young man, had left on her a definite impress. She wondered if ever she would meet him again, and wished ardently that she might. Her naiveté and utter lack of self-importance kept her from feeling piqued at his failure to hunt her up. She wondered often if life still seemed interesting to him, found herself borrowing a little of his high ardor. On the whole, her attitude toward "the adventure," as she loved to call it, was that of the little shepherdess and she brought back from that day only a mind "garlanded with pleasant memories."

Perhaps, she thought fancifully that Thursday evening,—the shepherdess meets the prince again and he gives her a position as court-artist. And she opened the little text to find out. But that lesson was never prepared, for Theophilus came in at that point with a bleeding gap in his head, caused by falling off a belated ice wagon. The sight of blood always made Mrs. Fetter sick, so Anna had the wound to clean and bind and Theophilus to soothe and get to bed.

So as it happened all she could do was to underline the new words and get their meaning from the vocabulary and trust to the gods that there would be no blind alleys in construction.

Anyone but Anna would have foreseen the end of that fairy-tale. For the prince, with the utter disregard for rank and wealth and training which so much fails to distinguish real princes, sought out the little shepherdess, who had been living most happily and unsuspectingly with her little sheep and her "so pleasant souvenirs" (so said Miss Selena Morton in translation), and besought her to marry him and live forever in his kingdom by the sea.

"'Oh, sky!' (thus ran Miss Morton's rendition for the French of 'Oh, heavens!'). 'Oh, sky!' exclaimed the shepherdess, and she told him she would accompany him all willingly, and when the prince had kissed her on both jaws they went on their way. And if you can find a happier ending of this history it is necessary that you go and tell it to the Pope at Rome." Thus, and not otherwise, did Miss Selena Morton mutilate that exquisite story!

But Miss Fetter was too amazed to care. Moreover, Tommy Reynolds and some of the other pupils had translated very well. Perhaps the work in grammar had been the best thing, after all—and perhaps she, too, was becoming a better teacher, she hoped to herself wistfully.

"I'm very much pleased with the work you've done to-day," she told the class. "It seems to me you've improved greatly—particularly Master Reynolds."

And Master Reynolds, who was cleaning the black-boards, smiled inscrutably.

All the way home Anna pondered on something new and sweet in her heart.

"But just think—the first part of the story had come true, why shouldn't the second? Oh, I wish, I wish—" She rushed into the "front-room," where Theophilus sat, his small broken head bandaged up, picking indefatigably at his banjo, and hugged him tumultuously.

He took her caress unmoved, having long ago decided that all women outside of aunts and mothers were crazy. "Look out, you'll break my new strings," he warned her. And she actually begged his pardon and proffered him fifteen cents towards the still visionary ukulele.

One can't go far on the similarity between one incident in one's life and the promise of a French fairy-tale. "Still things do happen," she told herself, surprised at her own tenacity. "Think of how Mr. Allen came into Mrs. Walton's that night and changed my whole life." She went to bed in a maze of rapture and anticipation.

Her mother was interested in a bazaar and dinner for the bazaar workers in the Methodist Church, but she had quarrelled with one of the sisters and she meant to go and arrange her booth and come back, so she shouldn't have to eat at the same table with that benighted Mrs. Vessels.

"I'd rather eat stalled oxen by myself all my days," she told her daughter Saturday morning, "than share the finest victuals at the same table as Pauline Vessels."

"Oh, mother," Anna had wailed, "how can you say such things? 'Stalled oxen' is the choice thing, the thing you are supposed to want to eat. You've got it upside down."

"Well, what difference does it make?" her mother had retorted, vexed for once. "I'm sure I shouldn't like the stuff, anyway. They'd probably be tough. Don't you let Philly stir out of this house till I come back, Anna. I don't want him to hurt hisself again. Do you think you can manage everything? I swept all the rooms yesterday but the kitchen. There's only that to scrub and the dusting to do."

Anna nodded. She was glad to be alone, glad to have work to do. She sent Theophilus out to clean up the side yard. She could hear him aimlessly pattering about.

"Ann," he called. She had finished scrubbing and all the dusting, too, except in the "front-room," which her mother *would* keep full of useless odds and ends—sheaves of wheat, silly bric-a-brac on whatnots. Ordinarily she hated it, but to-day—"to be alive"—her mind, not usually given to poetical flights, halted—"to be alive," no, "to be *young*," that was it, "to be young was very heaven." And he *had* said in the queerest way, "you didn't say she met a prince." If she could just find out something about him, who he was, where he lived, who *was* his mother's youngest sister. Why, what had she been thinking about to let two months go by without making any inquiry? True, she didn't know many colored people in Marytown, she had never bothered—she had been so concerned with her own affairs—but her mother knew everybody, positively, and a question here or there! Oh, if he only knew how the story ended! She became poetical again—"Would but some winged angel ere too late." She had to smile at that herself. Yet the winged angel was on the way in the person of Theophilus. He couldn't have adopted a more effective disguise.

"Ann," he called again. "C'n I go fishin' now with Tommy Reynolds? I've found all these nice worms in the garden, they'll make grand bait. Aunt (he pronounced it like the name of the humble insect) won't mind. She'd let me go 'n the air 'll be good for my head," he wheedled.

Anna, dusting the big Bible, hardly turned around. "No," she told him vigorously, "you can't go, Philly. You must stay till mother comes—she'll be here pretty soon, and you wash your hands and study your lessons a bit. Your last report was dreadful. Tommy Reynolds is only one year older than you and there he is in the second year of the seminary and you still in the graded schools. He plays, but he gets his lessons, too."

And then Theo began to rustle his wings, but neither he nor his cousin heard them.

"Oh, pshaw!" he retorted in disgust. "Tommy don't get no lessons. Someone around his house 's always helpin' him—he don't do nothin'. Why, his mother always does his drawin' for him."

"I don't know about his drawing," retorted his cousin, "but I know he does his French. He had a beautiful lesson yesterday. Don't laugh like that, Theophilus, it gets on my nerves."

For Theophilus was laughing shrilly, which perhaps drowned the still louder rustling of the wings.

"There you go," he jibbed, "there you go. He doesn't do his French at all, his uncle does it for him; he did it Thursday night when I was there. I heard him and I ain't tellin' any tales about it, neither," he put in, mistaking the look on her face, "for he said you'd be interested to have him do it for Tommy. He said he'd tell you about it the next time he saw you."

"Theophilus Jackson, you're crazy. I never saw Tommy Reynolds' uncle in my life. I don't even know where they live."

"Well, he's saw you," the child persisted and hesitated and looked puzzled—"though he did ask an awful lot of questions about you as if he didn't know you. Well, I don't know what he meant, but he did Tommy's French for him, I know that!" he ended in defiance.

Some faint prescience must have come to her mind, for she spoke with unwonted alertness. "He asked about me?" she insisted. "Sit down here, Theo, and tell me all about it. Who is his uncle?"

"Oh, I don't know, you needn't hold me so tight. I ain't goin' to go. Uncle Dick, Tommy calls him, Uncle Dick somethin'—oh—Winter—Mr. Richard Winter I heard Mrs. Reynolds call him. 'Now see here, Mr. Richard Winter,' she said to him—and she's his aunt, Anna, ain't that funny?—and he's bigger'n she and older, I guess, 'cause she looks awful young. I thought aunts were all old like Aunt Em."

She was sure now, and this miserable little boy had known all along. She alternately longed to shake him and hug him. She restrained both desires, knowing that the indulgence of either would dam the fount interminably.

"Go on, Philly," she begged him. "Maybe I can get Sid Williams to let you have the ukulele right away and you can pay him on the installment plan."

"Well, ain't I tellin' you? Tommy and me, we wanted to go to the movies and his mother said, 'No,' he'd got to get all his lessons first, and Tom winked at me and said he had 'em all, and his mother said, 'Not your French,' and Tommy said, 'Well, Uncle Dick's well again now, c'n I ask him to-night?' And just then his uncle walked in and said, 'Hullo, what's it all about?'—he talks so funny, Anna, and Tommy said, 'Please do my translation!' His mother said, 'Not till he's reviewed the first part; then, he hasn't seen the part for two months, because he's been studying something else.' And his uncle said, 'All right, hurry up, kid, because I must pack, I've got to go away again to-morrow.' And that was when Tommy's mother said, 'Well, Mr. Richard Winter, do you own the railway? Why don't you stay in one place? You've been here and gone again four times in the last two months!' And he said, 'Oh, Nora, I'm looking for something and I can't find it.' And she said, 'Did you lose it here?'—and he answered, awful sad, 'I think I did.' Why doesn't he buy another one, whatever it is, Cousin Anna?"

"I don't know, dear. Go on—did he say anything else?"

"Uh, huh—my but your face is red! And he said, 'Hit it up, Thomas-kid,' and Tommy opened the book and began to read all the silliest stuff about a lady in a park tending goats in a blue dress, and he said, his uncle did, 'What's that? What's that?' and he snatched the book away and looked at it, and he said in the funniest voice, 'I thought you said you were studyin' German all along. I never realized till this minute. Who's your teacher, Thomas?' And Tommy said *you* was. And he said, 'What does she look like?' Tommy said, 'She's awful cute, I must give her that, but she is too darn strict about her old crazy French,' and I said you was my cousin, and I told him not to get gay when he talked about you and if you was strict he needed it. And Mr. Winter said, 'Right-oh!' and asked me a lot of questions, and I said, no, you weren't pretty, but you were awful nice looking and had pretty skin and little feet, and he asked me did I ever spill a cup of cocoa in your lap."

She was on the floor now, her arms around him. "And what else, Philly. Oh, Philly, what else?"

"Lemme go, Ann, ain't I tellin' you?" He wriggled himself free. "Oh, yes, and then he said, 'Where does she live?' I said, 'With me, of course,' and he said, 'Here, in Marytown?' and I said, 'Yes, 37 Fortner street, near North,' and he said—oh, he swore, Ann—he said, 'My God, to think she's been here all this time. Here, boy, gimme that book,' and he sat down and started to read the old silly stuff to Tommy, and I ran out and jumped on the ice wagon and got my head busted. And will you get me the ukulele, Anna?"

She would, she assured him, get him anything, and he could go fishing and she would explain to Aunt Emmeline. "And here, take my apron upstairs with you. Why didn't you tell me before, Philly?"

"Well, what was there to tell, Anna?" he asked her, bewildered.

V

As soon as her mother should come in she'd bathe and dress and go out —but where? After all she was a girl, she must stand still, she didn't even know Mrs. Reynolds. But she could go by the house—yes, but he was to go away Friday, Theo said—why he *had* gone. Well, he would come back.

The gate clicked. At least, she could tell her mother. But she was crazy— she had only seen him once—well, so had the shepherdess seen the prince only once. Her mother would *have* to understand. What an age she was talking to one of those old Dorcas society sisters! She ran to the door and, of course, it was he on the steps, his hand just raised to knock.

Together they entered the room, silent, a little breathless. Even *he* was frightened. As for Anna—

"You knew I was coming," he told her. "I didn't find out until Thursday. Somehow I thought you lived in another town. You know you said the shepherdess had come such a long, long way, and I thought that meant you had too, and I was afraid to ask you. Oh, I've hunted and hunted, and Tommy, the rascal, told me he was crazy about German because he wanted some illustrated German books he saw in my trunk, and I thought he was studying it," he rushed on breathlessly. "And Thursday night I had to go right away to New York to be sure about something, before I dared to talk to you. And I'm to be a social settlement worker, and I can talk and talk and tell people about all those things," he ended lamely.

Anna stood silent.

"Anna, I thought, I hoped, I wondered"—he stammered. "Oh, do you think you could go with me—I want you so. And don't say you don't know me, we've always known each other, you lovely, brown child." His eyes entreated her.

But she still hung back. "You could talk to people about those wonderful things, but I, what could I do?"

"After the war," he explained to her, "we could go back to Europe and I could build bridges and you could draw the plans, and after we had made enough money we could come back and I could preach my gospel —for nothing."

"But, till then?"

"Till then" he whispered, "you could help me live that wonderful fairy-tale. Dear, I love you so"—and he kissed her tenderly, first on one cheek and then on the other.

"On both jaws," she whispered, a bit hysterically.

So then he kissed her on her perfect mouth.

Just then her mother, bidding Sister Pauline Vessels an amicable good-bye at the gate, came up the walk. So, hand in hand, they went to tell her about the happy ending.

MARY ELIZABETH

ILLUSTRATED BY LAURA WHEELER

Mary Elizabeth was late that morning. As a direct result, Roger left for work without telling me good-bye, and I spent most of the day fighting the headache which always comes if I cry.

For I cannot get a breakfast. I can manage a dinner,—one just puts the roast in the oven and takes it out again. And I really excel in getting lunch. There is a good delicatessen near us, and with dainty service and flowers, I get along very nicely. But breakfast! In the first place, it's a meal I neither like nor need. And I never, if I live a thousand years, shall learn to like coffee. I suppose that is why I cannot make it.

"Roger," I faltered, when the awful truth burst upon me and I began to realize that Mary Elizabeth wasn't coming, "Roger, couldn't you get breakfast downtown this morning? You know last time you weren't so satisfied with my coffee."

Roger was hostile. I think he had just cut himself, shaving. Anyway, he was horrid.

"No, I can't get my breakfast downtown!" He actually snapped at me. "Really, Sally, I don't believe there's another woman in the world who would send her husband out on a morning like this on an empty stomach. I don't see how you can be so unfeeling."

Well, it wasn't "a morning like this," for it was just the beginning of November. And I had only proposed his doing what I knew he would have to do eventually.

I didn't say anything more, but started on that breakfast. I don't know why I thought I had to have hot cakes! The breakfast really was awful! The cakes were tough and gummy and got cold one second, exactly, after I took them off the stove. And the coffee boiled, or stewed, or scorched, or did whatever the particular thing is that coffee shouldn't do. Roger sawed at one cake, took one mouthful of the dreadful brew, and pushed away his cup.

"It seems to me you might learn to make a decent cup of coffee," he said icily. Then he picked up his hat and flung out of the house.

I think it is stupid of me, too, not to learn how to make coffee. But, really, I'm no worse than Roger is about lots of things. Take "Five Hundred." Roger knows I love cards, and with the Cheltons right around the corner from us and as fond of it as I am, we could spend many a pleasant evening. But Roger will not learn. Only the night before, after I had gone through a whole hand with him, with hearts as trumps, I dealt the cards around again to imaginary opponents and we started playing. Clubs were trumps, and spades led. Roger, having no spades, played triumphantly a Jack of Hearts and proceeded to take the trick.

"But Roger," I protested, "you threw off."

"Well," he said, deeply injured, "didn't you say hearts were trumps when you were playing before?"

And when I tried to explain, he threw down the cards and wanted to know what difference it made; he'd rather play casino, anyway! I didn't go out and slam the door.

But I couldn't help from crying this particular morning. I not only value Roger's good opinion, but I hate to be considered stupid.

Mary Elizabeth came in about eleven o'clock. She is a small, weazened woman, very dark, somewhat wrinkled, and a model of self-possession. I wish I could make you see her, or that I could reproduce her accent, not that it is especially colored,—Roger's and mine are much more so—but her pronunciation, her way of drawing out her vowels, is so distinctively Mary Elizabethan!

I was ashamed of my red eyes and tried to cover up my embarrassment with sternness. "Mary Elizabeth," said I, "you are late!" Just as though she didn't know it.

"Yas'm, Mis' Pierson," she said, composedly, taking off her coat. She didn't remove her hat,—she never does until she has been in the house some two or three hours. I can't imagine why. It is a small, black, dusty affair, trimmed with black ribbon, some dingy white roses and a sheaf of wheat. I give Mary Elizabeth a dress and hat now and then, but, although I recognize the dress from time to time, I never see any change in the hat. I don't know what she does with my ex-millinery.

"Yas'm," she said again, and looked comprehensively at the untouched breakfast dishes and the awful viands, which were still where Roger had left them.

"Looks as though you'd had to git breakfast yoreself," she observed brightly. And went out in the kitchen and ate all those cakes and drank that unspeakable coffee! Really she did, and she didn't warm them up either. I watched her miserably, unable to decide whether Roger was too finicky or Mary Elizabeth a natural-born diplomat.

"Mr. Gales led me an awful chase last night," she explained. "When I got home yistiddy evenin', my cousin whut keeps house fer me (!) tole me Mr. Gales went out in the mornin' en hadn't come back."

"Mr. Gales," let me explain, is Mary Elizabeth's second husband, an octogenarian, and the most original person, I am convinced, in existence.

"Yas'm," she went on, eating a final cold hot-cake, "en I went to look fer 'im, en had the whole perlice station out all night huntin' 'im. Look like they wusn't never goin' to find 'im. But I ses, 'Jes' let me look fer enough en long enough en I'll find 'im,' I ses, en I did. Way out Georgy Avenue, with the hat on ole Mis' give 'im. Sent it to 'im all the way fum Chicaga. He's had it fifteen years,—high silk beaver. I knowed he wusn't goin' too fer with that hat on.

"I went up to 'im, settin' by a fence all muddy, holdin' his hat on with both hands. En I ses, 'Look here, man, you come erlong home with me, en let me put you to bed.' En he come jest as meek! No-o-me, I knowed he wusn't goin' fer with ole Mis' hat on."

"Who was old 'Mis,' Mary Elizabeth?" I asked her.

"Lady I used to work fer in Noo York," she informed me. "Me en Rosy, the cook, lived with her fer years. Ole Mis' was turrible fond of me, though her en Rosy used to querrel all the time. Jes' seemed like they couldn't git erlong. 'Member once Rosy run after her one Sunday with a knife, en I kep 'em apart. Reckon Rosy musta bin right put out with ole Mis' that day. By en by her en Rosy move to Chicaga, en when I married Mr. Gales, she sent 'im that hat. That old white woman shore did like me. It's so late, reckon I'd better put off sweepin' tel termorrer, ma'am."

I acquiesced, following her about from room to room. This was partly to get away from my own doleful thoughts—Roger really had hurt my feelings—but just as much to hear her talk. At first I used not to believe all she said, but after I investigated once and found her truthful in one amazing statement, I capitulated.

She had been telling me some remarkable tale of her first husband and I was listening with the stupefied attention, to which she always reduces me. Remember she was speaking of her first husba znd.

"En I ses to 'im. I ses, 'Mr Gale—'"

"Wait a moment, Mary Eiizabeth," I interrupted, meanly delighted to have caught her for once. "You mean your first husband, don't you?"

"Yas'm," she replied. "En I ses to 'im, 'Mr. Gale! I ses—'"

"But, Mary Elizabeth," I persisted, "that's your second husband, isn't it,—Mr. Gale?"

She gave me her long-drawn "No-o-me! My first husband was Mr. Gale and my second is Mr. *Gales*. He spells his name with a Z, I reckon. I ain't never see it writ. Ez I wus sayin', I ses to Mr. Gale—"

And it was true! Since then I have never doubted Mary Elizabeth.

She was loquacious that afternoon. She told me about her sister, "where's got a home in the country and where's got eight children." I used to read Lucy Pratt's stories about little Ephraim or Ezekiel, I forget his name, who always said "where's" instead of "who's," but I never believed it really till I heard Mary Elizabeth use it. For some reason or other she never mentions her sister without mentioning the home, too. "My sister where's got a home in the country" is her unvarying phrase.

"Mary Elizabeth," I asked her once, "does your sister live in the country, or does she simply own a house there?"

"Yas'm," she told me.

She is fond of her sister. "If Mr. Gales wus to die," she told me complacently, "I'd go to live with her."

"If he should die," I asked her idly, "would you marry again?"

"Oh, no-o-me!" She was emphatic. "Though I don't know why I shouldn't, I'd come by it hones'. My father wus married four times."

That shocked me out of my headache. "Four times, Mary Elizabeth, and you had all those step-mothers!" My mind refused to take it in.

"Oh, no-o-me! I always lived with mamma. She was his first wife."

I hadn't thought of people in the state in which I had instinctively placed Mary Elizabeth's father and mother as indulging in divorce, but as Roger says slangily, "I wouldn't know."

Mary Elizabeth took off the dingy hat. "You see, papa and mamma—" the ineffable pathos of hearing this woman of sixty-four, with a husband of eighty, use the old childish terms!

"Papa and mamma wus slaves, you know, Mis' Pierson, and so of course they wusn't exackly married. White folks wouldn't let 'em. But they wus awf'ly in love with each other. Heard mamma tell erbout it lots of times, and how papa wus the han'somest man! Reckon she wus long erbout sixteen or seventeen then. So they jumped over a broomstick, en they wus jes as happy! But not long after I come erlong, they sold papa down South, and mamma never see him no mo' fer years and years. Thought he was dead. So she married again."

"And he came back to her, Mary Elizabeth?" I was overwhelmed with the woefulness of it.

"Yas'm. After twenty-six years. Me and my sister where's got a home in the country—she's really my half-sister, see Mis' Pierson,—

her en mamma en my step-father en me wus all down in Bumpus, Virginia, workin' fer some white folks, and we used to live in a little cabin, had a front stoop to it. En one day an ole cullud man come by, had a lot o' whiskers. I'd saw him lots of times there in Bumpus, lookin' and peerin' into every cullud woman's face. En jes' then my sister she call out,

'Come here, you Ma'y Elizabeth,' en that old man stopped, en he looked at me en he looked at me, en he ses to me, 'Chile, is yo' name Ma'y Elizabeth?'

"You know, Mis' Pierson, I thought he was jes' bein' fresh, en I ain't paid no 'tention to 'im. I ain't sed nuthin' ontel he spoke to me three or four times, en then I ses to 'im, 'Go 'way fum here, man, you ain't got no call to be fresh with me. I'm a decent woman. You'd oughta be ashamed of yoreself, an ole man like you.'"

Mary Elizabeth stopped and looked hard at the back of her poor wrinkled hands.

"En he says to me, 'Daughter,' he ses, jes' like that, 'daughter,' he ses, 'hones' I ain't bein' fresh. Is yo' name shore enough Ma'y Elizabeth?'

"En I tole him, 'Yas'r.'

"'Chile,' he ses, 'whar is yo' daddy?'

"'Ain't got no daddy,' I tole him peart-like. 'They done tuk 'im away fum me twenty-six years ago. I wusn't but a mite of a baby. Sol' 'im down the river. My mother often talks about it.' And, oh, Mis' Pierson, you shoulda see the glory come into his face!

"'Yore mother!' he ses kinda out of breath, 'yore mother! Ma'y Elizabeth, whar is your mother?'"

'Back thar on the stoop,' I tole 'im. 'Why, did you know my daddy?'

"But he didn't pay no 'tention to me, jes' turned and walked up the stoop whar mamma was settin'! She wus feelin' sorta porely that day. En you oughta see me steppin' erlong after 'im.

"He walked right up to her and giv' her one look. 'Oh, Maggie,' he shout out, 'oh, Maggie! Ain't you know me? Maggie, ain't you know me?'

"Mamma look at 'im and riz up outa her cheer. 'Who're you?' she ses kinda trimbly, callin' me Maggie thata way? Who're you?'

"He went up real close to her, then, 'Maggie,' he ses, jes like that, kinda sad 'n tender, 'Maggie!' And hel' out his arms.

"She walked right into them. 'Oh,' she ses, 'it's Cassius! It's Cassius! It's my husban' come back to me! It's Cassius!' They wus like two mad people.

"My sister Minnie and me, we jes' stood and gawped at 'em. There they wus, holding on to each other like two pitiful childrun, en he tuk her hands and kissed 'em.

"'Maggie,' he ses, you'll come away with me, won't you? You gona take me back, Maggie? We'll go away, you en Ma'y Elizabeth en me. Won't we, Maggie?'

"Reckon my mother clean fergot my step-father. 'Yes, Cassius,' she ses, 'we'll go away.' And then she sees Minnie, en it all comes back to her. 'Oh, Cassius,' she ses, 'I cain't go with you, I'm married again, en this time fer real. This here gal's mine and three boys, too, and another chile comin' in November!'"

"But she went with him, Mary Elizabeth," I pleaded. "Surely she went with him after all those years. He really was her husband."

I don't know whether Mary Elizabeth meant to be sarcastic or not. "Oh, no-o-me, mamma couldn't a done that. She wus a good woman. Her ole master, whut done sol' my father down river, brung her up too religious fer that, en anyways, papa was married again, too. Had his fourth wife there in Bumpus with 'im."

The unspeakable tragedy of it!

I left her and went up to my room, and hunted out my dark-blue serge dress which I had meant to wear again that winter. But I had to give Mary Elizabeth something, so I took the dress down to her.

She was delighted with it. I could tell she was, because she used her rare and untranslatable expletive.

"Haytian!" she said. "My sister where's got a home in the country, got a dress looks somethin' like this, but it ain't as good. No-o-me. She got hers to wear at a friend's weddin',—gal she was riz up with. Thet gal married well, too, lemme tell you; her husband's a Sunday School sup'rintender."

I told her she needn't wait for Mr. Pierson, I would put dinner on the table. So off she went in the gathering dusk, trudging bravely back to her Mr. Gales and his high silk hat.

I watched her from the window till she was out of sight. It had been such a long time since I had thought of slavery. I was born in Pennsylvania, and neither my parents nor grandparents had been slaves; otherwise I might have had the same tale to tell as Mary Elizabeth, or worse yet, Roger and I might have lived in those black days and loved and lost each other and futilely, damnably, met again like Cassius and Maggie.

Whereas it was now, and I had Roger and Roger had me.

How I loved him as I sat there in the hazy dusk. I thought of his dear, bronze perfection, his habit of swearing softly in excitement, his blessed stupidity. Just the same I didn't meet him at the door as usual, but pretended to be busy. He came rushing to me with the *Saturday Evening Post*, which is more to me than rubies. I thanked him warmly, but aloofly, if you can get that combination.

We ate dinner almost in silence for my part. But he praised everything,—the cooking, the table, my appearance.

After dinner we went up to the little sitting-room. He hoped I wasn't tired,—couldn't he fix the pillows for me? So!

I opened the magazine and the first thing I saw was a picture of a woman gazing in stony despair at the figure of a man disappearing around the bend of the road. It was too much. Suppose that were Roger and I! I'm afraid I sniffled. He was at my side in a moment.

"Dear loveliest! Don't cry. It was all my fault. You aren't any worse about coffee than I am about cards! And anyway, I needn't have slammed the door! Forgive me, Sally. I always told you I was hard to get along with. I've had a horrible day,—don't stay cross with me, dearest."

I held him to me and sobbed outright on his shoulder. "It isn't you, Roger," I told him, "I'm crying about Mary Elizabeth."

I regret to say he let me go then, so great was his dismay. Roger will never be half the diplomat that Mary Elizabeth is.

"Holy smokes!" he groaned. "She isn't going to leave us for good, is she?"

So then I told him about Maggie and Cassius. "And oh, Roger," I ended futilely, "to think that they had to separate after all those years, when he had come back, old and with whiskers!" I didn't mean to be so banal, but I was crying too hard to be coherent.

Roger had got up and was walking the floor, but he stopped then aghast.

"Whiskers!" he moaned. "My hat! Isn't that just like a woman?" He had to clear his throat once or twice before he could go on, and I think he wiped his eyes.

"Wasn't it the—" I really can't say what Roger said here,—"wasn't it the darndest hard luck that when he did find her again, she should be married? She might have waited."

I stared at him astounded. "But, Roger," I reminded him, "he had married three other times, he didn't wait."

"Oh—!" said Roger, unquotably, "married three fiddlesticks! He only did that to try to forget her."

Then he came over and knelt beside me again. "Darling, I do think it is a sensible thing for a poor woman to learn how to cook, but I don't care as long as you love me and we are together. Dear loveliest, if I had been Cassius,—he caught my hands so tight that he hurt them,—and I had married fifty times and had come back and found you married to someone else, I'd have killed you, killed you."

Well, he wasn't logical, but he was certainly convincing.

So thus, and not otherwise, Mary Elizabeth healed the breach.

THE SLEEPER WAKES

ILLUSTRATED BY LAURA WHEELER

A NOVELETTE IN THREE INSTALLMENTS

Amy recognized the incident as the beginning of one of her phases. Always from a child she had been able to tell when "something was going to happen." She had been standing in Marshall's store, her young, eager gaze intent on the lovely little sample dress which was not from Paris, but quite as dainty as anything that Paris could produce. It was not the lines or even the texture that fascinated Amy so much, it was the grouping of colors—of shades. She knew the combination was just right for her.

"Let me slip it on, Miss," said the saleswoman suddenly. She had nothing to do just then, and the girl was so evidently charmed and so pretty—it was a pleasure to wait on her.

"Oh no," Amy had stammered. "I haven't time." She had already wasted two hours at the movies, and she knew at home they were waiting for her.

The saleswoman slipped the dress over the girl's pink blouse, and tucked the linen collar under so as to bring the edge of the dress next to her pretty neck. The dress was apricot-color shading into a shell pink and the shell pink shaded off again into the pearl and pink whiteness of Amy's skin. The saleswoman beamed as Amy, entranced, surveyed herself naively in the tall looking-glass.

Then it was that the incident befell. Two men walking idly through the dress-salon stopped and looked—she made an unbelievably pretty picture. One of them with a short, soft brown beard,—"fuzzy" Amy thought to herself as she caught his glance in the mirror—spoke to his companion.

"Jove, how I'd like to paint her!" But it was the look on the other man's face that caught her and thrilled her. "My God! Can't a girl be beautiful!" he said half to himself. The pair passed on.

Amy stepped out of the dress and thanked the saleswoman half absently. She wanted to get home and think, think to herself about that look. She had seen it before in men's eyes, it had been in the eyes of the men in the moving-picture which she had seen that afternoon. But she had not thought *she* could cause it. Shut up in her little room she pondered over it. Her beauty,—she was really good-looking then—she could stir people —men! A girl of seventeen has no psychology, she does not go beneath the surface, she accepts. But she knew she was entering on one of her phases.

She was always living in some sort of story. She had started it when as a child of five she had driven with the tall, proud, white woman to Mrs. Boldin's home. Mrs. Boldin was a bride of one year's standing then. She was slender and very, very comely, with her rich brown skin and her hair that crinkled thick and soft above a low forehead. The house was still redolent of new furniture; Mr. Boldin was spick and span—he, unlike the furniture, remained so for that matter. The white woman had told Amy that this henceforth was to be her home.

Amy was curious, fond of adventure; she did not cry. She did not, of course, realize that she was to stay here indefinitely, but if she had, even at that age she would hardly have shed tears, she was always too eager, too curious to know, to taste what was going to happen next. Still since she had had almost no dealings with colored people and knew absolutely none of the class to which Mrs. Boldin belonged, she did venture one question.

"Am I going to be colored now?"

The tall white woman had flushed and paled. "You—" she began, but the words choked her. "Yes, you are going to be colored now," she ended finally. She was a proud woman, in a moment she had recovered her usual poise. Amy carried with her for many years the memory of that proud head. She never saw her again.

When she was sixteen she asked Mrs. Boldin the question which in the light of that memory had puzzled her always. "Mrs. Boldin, tell me—am I white or colored?"

And Mrs. Boldin had told her and told her truly that she did not know.

"A—a—mee!" Mrs. Boldin's voice mounted on the last syllable in a shrill crescendo. Amy rose and went downstairs.

Down in the comfortable, but rather shabby dining-room which the Boldins used after meals to sit in, Mr. Boldin, a tall black man, with aristocratic features, sat reading; little Cornelius Boldin sat practicing on a cornet, and Mrs. Boldin sat rocking. In all of their eyes was the manifestation of the light that Amy loved, but how truly she loved it, she was not to guess till years later.

"Amy," Mrs. Boldin paused in her rocking, "did you get the braid?" Of course she had not, though that was the thing she had gone to Marshall's for. Amy always forgot essentials. If she went on an errand, and she always went willingly, it was for the pure joy of going. Who knew what angels might meet one unawares? Not that Amy thought in biblical or in literary phrases. She was in the High School, it is true, but she was simply passing through, "getting by" she would have said carelessly. The only reading that had ever made any impression on her had been fairy tales read to her in those long remote days when she had lived with the tall, proud woman; and descriptions in novels or histories of beautiful, stately palaces tenanted by beautiful, stately women. She could pore over such pages for hours, her face flushed, her eyes eager.

At present she cast about for an excuse. She had so meant to get the braid. "There was a dress—" she began lamely, she was never deliberately dishonest.

Mr. Boldin cleared his throat and nervously fingered his paper. Cornelius ceased his awful playing and blinked at her shortsightedly through his thick glasses. Both of these, the man and the little boy, loved the beautiful, inconsequent creature with her airy, irresponsible ways. But Mrs. Boldin loved her too, and because she loved her she could not scold.

"Huh! I don't want to look at no pretty girl!"

"Of course you forgot," she began chidingly. Then she smiled. "There was a dress that you looked at *perhaps*. But confess, didn't you go to the movies first?"

Yes, Amy confessed she had done just that. "And oh, Mrs. Boldin, it was the most wonderful picture—a girl—such a pretty one—and she was poor, awfully. And somehow she met the most wonderful people and they were so kind to her. And she married a man who was just tremendously rich and he gave her everything. I did so want Cornelius to see it."

"Huh!" said Cornelius who had been listening not because he was interested, but because he wanted to call Amy's attention to his playing as soon as possible. "Huh! I don't want to look at no pretty girl. Did they have anybody looping the loop in an airship?"

"You'd better stop seeing pretty girl pictures, Amy," said Mr. Boldin kindly. "They're not always true to life. Besides, I know where you can see all the pretty girls you want without bothering to pay twenty-five cents for it."

Amy smiled at the implied compliment and went on happily studying her lessons. They were all happy in their own way. Amy because she was sure of their love and admiration, Mr. and Mrs. Boldin because of her beauty and innocence and Cornelius because he knew he had in his foster-sister a listener whom his terrible practicing could never bore. He played brokenly a piece he had found in an old music-book. *"There's an aching void in every heart, brother."*

"Where *do* you pick up those old things, Neely?" said his mother fretfully. But Amy could not have her favorite's feelings injured.

"I think it's lovely," she announced defensively. "Cornelius, I'll ask Sadie Murray to lend me her brother's book. He's learning the cornet, too, and you can get some new pieces. Oh, isn't it awful to have to go to bed? Good-night, everybody." She smiled her charming, ever ready smile, the mere reflex of youth and beauty and content.

"You do spoil her, Mattie," said Mr. Boldin after she had left the room. "She's only seventeen—here, Cornelius, you go to bed—but it seems to me she ought to be more dependable about errands. Though she is splendid about some things," he defended her. "Look how willingly she goes off to bed. She'll be asleep before she knows it when most girls of her age would want to be in the street."

But upstairs Amy was far from sleep. She lit one gas-jet and pulled down the shades. Then she stuffed tissue paper in the keyhole and under the doors, and lit the remaining gas-jets. The light thus thrown on the mirror of the ugly oak dresser was perfect. She slipped off the pink blouse and found two scarfs, a soft yellow and a soft pink,—she had had them in a scarf-dance for a school entertainment. She wound them and draped them about her pretty shoulders and loosened her hair. In the mirror she apostrophized the beautiful, glowing vision of herself.

"There", she said, "I'm like the girl in the picture. She had nothing but her beautiful face—and she did so want to be happy." She sat down on the side of the rather lumpy bed and stretched out her arms. "I want to be happy, too." She intoned it earnestly, almost like an incantation. "I want wonderful clothes, and people around me, men adoring me, and the world before me. I want—everything! It will come, it will all come because I want it so." She sat frowning intently as she was apt to do when very much engrossed. "And we'd all be so happy. I'd give Mr. and Mrs. Boldin money! And Cornelius—he'd go to college and learn all about his old airships. Oh, if I only knew how to begin!"

Smiling, she turned off the lights and crept to bed.

II

Quite suddenly she knew she was going to run away. That was in October. By December she had accomplished her purpose. Not that she was the least bit unhappy but because she must get out in the world,—she felt caged, imprisoned. "Trenton is stifling me," she would have told you, in her unconsciously adopted "movie" diction. New York she knew was the place for her. She had her plans all made. She had sewed steadily after school for two months—as she frequently did when she wanted to buy her season's wardrobe, so besides her carfare she had $25. She went immediately to a white Y. W. C. A., stayed there two nights, found and answered an advertisement for clerk and waitress in a small confectionery and bakery-shop, was accepted and there she was launched.

Perhaps it was because of her early experience when as a tiny child she was taken from that so different home and left at Mrs. Boldin's, perhaps it was some fault in her own disposition, concentrated and egotistic as she was, but certainly she felt no pangs of separation, no fear of her future. She was cold too,—unfired though so to speak rather than icy,—and fastidious. This last quality kept her safe where morality or religion, of neither of which had she any conscious endowment, would have availed her nothing. Unbelievably then she lived two years in New York, unspoiled, untouched, going to her work on the edge of Greenwich Village early and coming back late, knowing almost no one and yet altogether happy in the expectation of something wonderful, which she knew some day must happen.

It was at the end of the second year that she met Zora Harrisson. Zora used to come into lunch with a group of habitués of the place—all of them artists and writers as Amy gathered. Mrs. Harrisson (for she was married as Amy later learned) appealed to the girl because she knew so well how to afford the contrast to her blonde, golden beauty. Purple, dark and regal, developed in velvets and heavy silks, and strange marine blues she wore, and thus made Amy absolutely happy. Singularly enough, the girl, intent as she was on her own life and experiences, had felt up to this time no yearning to know these strange, happy beings who surrounded her. She did miss Cornelius, but otherwise she was never lonely, or if she was she hardly knew it, for she had always lived an inner life to herself. But Mrs. Harrisson magnetized her—she could not keep her eyes from her face, from her wonderful clothes. She made conjectures about her.

The wonderful lady came in late one afternoon—an unusual thing for her. She smiled at Amy invitingly, asked some banal questions and their first conversation began. The acquaintance once struck up progressed rapidly—after a few weeks Mrs. Harrisson invited the girl to come to see her. Amy accepted quietly, unaware that anything extraordinary was happening. Zora noticed this and liked it. She had an apartment in 12th Street in a house inhabited only by artists—she was no mean one herself. Amy was fascinated by the new world into which she found herself ushered; Zora's surroundings were very beautiful and Zora herself was a study. She opened to the girl's amazed vision fields of thought and conjecture, phases of whose existence Amy, who was a builder of phases, had never dreamed. Zora had been a poor girl of good family. She had wanted to study art, she had deliberately married a rich man and as deliberately obtained in the course of four years a divorce, and she was now living in New York studying by means of her alimony and enjoying to its fullest the life she loved. She took Amy on a footing with herself—the girl's refinement, her beauty, her interest in colors (though this in Amy at that time was purely sporadic, never consciously encouraged), all this gave Zora a figure about which to plan and build a romance. Amy had told her the truth, but not all about her coming to New York. She had grown tired of Trenton—her people were all dead—the folks with whom she lived were kind and good but not "inspiring" (she had borrowed the term from Zora and it was true, the Boldins, when one came to think of it, were not "inspiring"), so she had run away.

Zora had gone into raptures. "What an adventure! My dear, the world is yours. Why, with your looks and your birth, for I suppose you really belong to the Kildares who used to live in Philadelphia, I think there was a son who ran off and married an actress or someone—they disowned him I remember,—you can reach any height. You must marry a wealthy man—perhaps someone who is interested in art and who will let you pursue your studies." She insisted always that Amy had run away in order to study art. "But luck like that comes to few," she sighed, remembering her own plight, for Mr. Harrisson had been decidedly unwilling to let her pursue her studies, at least to the extent she wished. "Anyway you must marry wealth,—one can always get a divorce," she ended sagely.

Amy—she came to Zora's every night now—used to listen dazedly at first. She had accepted willingly enough Zora's conjecture about her birth, came to believe it in fact—but she drew back somewhat at such wholesale exploitation of people to suit one's own convenience, still she did not probe too far into this thought—nor did she grasp at all the infamy of exploitation of self. She ventured one or two objections, however, but Zora brushed everything aside.

"Everybody is looking out for himself," she said airily. "I am interested in you, for instance, not for philanthropy's sake, but because I am lonely, and you are charming and pretty and don't get tired of hearing me talk. You'd better come and live with me awhile, my dear, six months or a year. It doesn't cost any more for two than for one, and you can always leave when we get tired of each other. A girl like you can always get a job. If you are worried about being dependent you can pose for me and design my frocks, and oversee Julienne"—her maid-of-all-work—"I'm sure she's a stupendous robber."

Amy came, not at all overwhelmed by the good luck of it—good luck was around the corner more or less for everyone, she supposed. Moreover, she was beginning to absorb some of Zora's doctrine—she, too, must look out for herself. Zora *was* lonely, she *did* need companionship; Julienne was careless about change and odd blouses and left-over dainties. Amy had her own sense of honor. She carried out faithfully her share of the bargain, cut down waste, renovated Zora's clothes, posed for her, listened to her endlessly and bore with her fitfulness. Zora was truly grateful for this last. She was temperamental but Amy had good nerves and her strong natural inclination to let people do as they wanted stood her in good stead. She was a little stolid, a little unfeeling under her lovely exterior. Her looks at this time belied her—her perfect ivory-pink face, her deep luminous eyes,—very brown they were with purple depths that made one think of pansies—her charming, rather wide mouth, her whole face set in a frame of very soft, very live, brown hair which grew in wisps and tendrils and curls and waves back from her smooth, young forehead. All this made one look for softness and ingenuousness. The ingenuousness was there, but not the softness—except of her fresh, vibrant loveliness.

On the whole then she progressed famously with Zora. Sometimes the latter's callousness shocked her, as when they would go strolling through the streets south of Washington Square. The children, the people all foreign, all dirty, often very artistic, always immensely human, disgusted Zora except for "local color"—she really could reproduce them wonderfully. But she almost hated them for being what they were.

"Br-r-r, dirty little brats!" she would say to Amy. "Don't let them touch me." She was frequently amazed at her protégée's utter indifference to their appearance, for Amy herself was the pink of daintiness. They were turning from MacDougall into Bleecker Street one day and Amy had patted a child—dirty, but lovely—on the head.

"They are all people just like anybody else, just like you and me, Zora," she said in answer to her friend's protest.

"You *are* the true democrat," Zora returned with a shrug. But Amy did not understand her.

Not the least of Amy's services was to come between Zora and the too pressing attention of the men who thronged about her.

"Oh, go and talk to Amy," Zora would say, standing slim and gorgeous in some wonderful evening gown. She was an extraordinarily attractive creature, very white and pink, with great ropes of dazzling gold hair, and that look of no-age which only American women possess. As a matter of fact she was thirty-nine, immensely sophisticated and selfish, even, Amy thought, a little cruel. Her present mode of living just suited her; she could not stand any condition that bound her, anything at all *exigeant*. It was useless for anyone to try to influence her. If she did not want to talk, she would not.

The men used to obey her orders and seek Amy sulkily at first, but afterwards with considerably more interest. She was so lovely to look at. But they really, as Zora knew, preferred to talk to the older woman, for while with Zora indifference was a rôle, second nature by now but still a rôle—with Amy it was natural and she was also a trifle shallow. She had the admiration she craved, she was comfortable, she asked no more. Moreover she thought the men, with the exception of Stuart James Wynne, rather uninteresting—they were faddists for the most part, crazy not about art or music, but merely about some phase such as cubism or syncopation.

Wynne, who was much older than the other half-dozen men who weekly paid Zora homage—impressed her by his suggestion of power. He was a retired broker, immensely wealthy (Zora, who had known him since childhood, informed her), very set and purposeful and very polished. He was perhaps fifty-five, widely traveled, of medium height, very white skin and clear, frosty, blue eyes, with sharp, proud features. He liked Amy from the beginning, her childishness touched him. In particular he admired her pliability—not knowing it was really indifference. He had been married twice; one wife had divorced him, the other had died. Both marriages were unsuccessful owing to his dominant, rather unsympathetic nature. But he had softened considerably with years, though he still had decided views, was glad to see that Amy, in spite of Zora's influence, neither smoked nor drank. He liked her shallowness—she fascinated him.

Zora had told him much—just the kind of romantic story to appeal to the rich, powerful man. Here was beauty forlorn, penniless, of splendid birth,—for Zora once having connected Amy with the Philadelphia Kildares never swerved from that belief. Amy seemed to Wynne everything a girl should be—she was so unspoiled, so untouched. He asked her to marry him. If she had tried she could not have acted more perfectly. She looked at him with her wonderful eyes.

"But I am poor, ignorant—a nobody," she stammered. "I'm afraid I don't love you either," she went on in her pretty troubled voice, "though I do like you very, very much."

He liked her honesty and her self-depreciation, even her coldness. The fact that she was not flattered seemed to him an extra proof of her native superiority. He, himself, was a representative of one of the South's oldest families, though he had lived abroad lately.

"I have money and influence," he told her gravely, "but I count them nothing without you." And as for love—he would teach her that, he ended, his voice shaking a little. Underneath all his chilly, polished exterior he really cared.

"It seems an unworthy thing to say," he told her wistfully, for she seemed very young beside his experienced fifty-five years, "but anything you wanted in this world could be yours. I could give it to you,—clothes, houses and jewels."

"Don't be an idiot," Zora had said when Amy told her. "Of course, marry him. He'll give you a beautiful home and position. He's probably no harder to get along with than anybody else, and if he is, there is always the divorce court."

It seemed to Amy somehow that she was driving a bargain—how infamous a one she could not suspect. But Zora's teachings had sunk deep.

Wynne loved her, and he could secure for her what she wanted. "And after all," she said to herself once, "it really is my dream coming true."

She resolved to marry him. There were two weeks of delirious, blissful shopping. Zora was very generous. It seemed to Amy that the whole world was contributing largesse to her happiness. She was to have just what she wanted and as her taste was perfect she afforded almost as much pleasure to the people from whom she bought as to herself. In particular she brought rapture to an exclusive modiste in Forty-second Street who exclaimed at her "so perfect taste".

"Mademoiselle is of a marvellous, of an absolute correctness," she said.

Everything whirled by. After the shopping there was the small, impressive wedding. Amy stumbled somehow through the service, struck by its awful solemnity. Then later there was the journey and the big house waiting them in the small town, fifty miles south of Richmond. Wynne was originally from Georgia, but business and social interests had made it necessary for him to be nearer Washington and New York.

Amy was absolute mistress of himself and his home, he said, his voice losing its coldness. "Ah, my dear, you'll never realize what you mean to me—I don't envy any other man in the world. You are so beautiful, so sweet, so different!"

III

From the very beginning he was different from what she had supposed. To start with he was far, far wealthier, and he had, too, a tradition, a family-pride which to Amy was inexplicable. Still more inexplicably he had a race-pride. To his wife this was not only strange but foolish. She was as Zora had once suggested, the true democrat. Not that she preferred the company of her maids, though the reason for this did not lie per se in the fact that they were maids. There was simply no common ground. But she was uniformly kind, a trait which had she been older would have irritated her husband. As it was, he saw in it only an additional indication of her freshness, her lack of worldliness which seemed to him the attributes of an inherent refinement and goodness untouched by experience.

He, himself, was intolerant of all people of inferior birth or standing and looked with contempt on foreigners, except the French and English. All the rest were variously "guineys", "niggers", and "wops", and all of them he genuinely despised and hated, and talked of them with the huge intolerant carelessness characteristic of occidental civilization. Amy was never able to understand it. People were always first and last, just people to her. Growing up as the average colored American girl does grow up, surrounded by types of every hue, color and facial configuration she had had no absolute ideal. She was not even aware that there was one. Wynne, who in his grim way had a keen sense of humor, used to be vastly amused at the artlessness with which she let him know that she did not consider him good-looking. She never wanted him to wear anything but dark blue, or sombre mixtures always.

"They take away from that awful whiteness of your skin," she used to tell him, "and deepen the blue of your eyes."

In the main she made no attempt to understand him, as indeed she made no attempt to understand anything. The result, of course, was that such ideas as seeped into her mind stayed there, took growth and later bore fruit. But just at this period she was like a well-cared for, sleek, house-pet, delicately nurtured, velvety, content to let her days pass by. She thought almost nothing of her art just now, except as her sensibilities were jarred by an occasional disharmony. Likewise, even to herself, she never criticized Wynne, except when some act or attitude of his stung. She could never understand why he, so fastidious, so versed in elegance of word and speech, so careful in his surroundings, even down to the last detail of glass and napery, should take such evident pleasure in literature of a certain prurient type. He fairly revelled in the realistic novels which to her depicted sheer badness. He would get her to read to him, partly because he liked to be read to, mostly because he enjoyed the realism and in a slighter degree because he enjoyed seeing her shocked. Her point of view amused him.

"What funny people," she would say naively, "to do such things." She could not understand the liaisons and intrigues of women in the society novels, such infamy was stupid and silly. If one starved, it was conceivable that one might steal; if one were intentionally injured, one might hit back, even murder; but deliberate nastiness she could not envisage. The stories, after she had read them to him, passed out of her mind as completely as though they had never existed.

Picture the two of them spending three years together with practically no friction. To his dominance and intolerance she opposed a soft and unobtrusive indifference. What she wanted she had, ease, wealth, adoration, love, too, passionate and imperious, but she had never known any other kind. She was growing cleverer also, her knowledge of French was increasing, she was acquiring a knowledge of politics, of commerce and of the big social questions, for Wynne's interests were exhaustive and she did most of his reading for him. Another woman might have yearned for a more youthful companion, but her native coldness kept her content. She did not love him, she had never really loved anybody, but little Cornelius Boldin—he had been such an enchanting, such a darling baby, she remembered,—her heart contracted painfully when she thought as she did very often of his warm softness.

"He must be a big boy now," she would think almost maternally, wondering—once she had been so sure!—if she would ever see him again. But she was very fond of Wynne, and he was crazy over her just as Zora had predicted. He loaded her with gifts, dresses, flowers, jewels—she amused him because none but colored stones appealed to her.

"Diamonds are so hard, so cold, and pearls are dead," she told him.

Nothing ever came between them, but his ugliness, his hatefulness to dependents. It hurt her so, for she was naturally kind in her careless, uncomprehending way. True, she had left Mrs. Boldin without a word, but she did not guess how completely Mrs. Boldin loved her. She would have been aghast had she realized how stricken her flight had left them. At twenty-two, Amy was still as good, as unspoiled, as pure as a child. Of course with all this she was too unquestioning, too selfish, too vain, but they were all faults of her lovely, lovely flesh. Wynne's intolerance finally got on her nerves. She used to blush for his unkindness. All the servants were colored, but she had long since ceased to think that perhaps she, too, was colored, except when he, by insult toward an employee, overt always at least implied, made her realize his contemptuous dislike and disregard for a dark skin or Negro blood.

"Stuart, how can you say such things?" she would expostulate. "You can't expect a man to stand such language as that." And Wynne would sneer, "A man—you don't consider a nigger a man, do you? Oh, Amy, don't be such a fool. You've got to keep them in their places."

Some innate sense of the fitness of things kept her from condoling outspokenly with the servants, but they knew she was ashamed of her husband's ways. Of course, they left—it seemed to Amy that Peter, the butler, was always getting new "help",—but most of the upper servants stayed, for Wynne paid handsomely and although his orders were meticulous and insistent, the retinue of employees was so large that the individual's work was light.

Most of the servants who did stay on in spite of Wynne's occasional insults had a purpose in view. Callie, the cook, Amy found out, had two children at Howard University—of course she never came in contact with Wynne—the chauffeur had a crippled sister. Rose, Amy's maid and purveyor of much outside information, was the chief support of her family. About Peter, Amy knew nothing; he was a striking, taciturn man, very competent, who had left the Wynnes' service years before and had returned in Amy's third year. Wynne treated him with comparative respect. But Stephen, the new valet, met with entirely different treatment. Amy's heart yearned toward him, he was like Cornelius, with short-sighted, patient eyes, always willing, a little over-eager. Amy recognized him for what he was; a boy of respectable, ambitious parentage, striving for the means for an education; naturally far above his present calling, yet willing to pass through all this as a means to an end. She questioned Rosa about him.

"Oh, Stephen," Rosa told her, "yes'm, he's workin' for fair. He's got a brother at the Howard's and a sister at Smith's. Yes'm, it do seem a little hard on him, but Stephen, he say, they're both goin' to turn roun' and help him when they get through. That blue silk has a rip in it, Miss Amy, if you was thinkin' of wearin' that. Yes'm, somehow I don't think Steve's very strong, kinda worries like. I guess he's sorta nervous."

Amy told Wynne. "He's such a nice boy, Stuart," she pleaded, "it hurts me to have you so cross with him. Anyway don't call him names." She was both surprised and frightened at the feeling in her that prompted her to interfere. She had held so aloof from other people's interests all these years.

"I *am* colored," she told herself that night. "I feel it inside of me. I must be or I couldn't care so about Stephen. Poor boy, I suppose Cornelius is just like him. I wish Stuart would let him alone. I wonder if all white people are like that. Zora was hard, too, on unfortunate people." She pondered over it a bit. "I wonder what Stuart would say if he knew I was colored?" She lay perfectly still, her smooth brow knitted, thinking hard. "But he loves me," she said to herself still silently. "He'll always love my looks," and she fell to thinking that all the wonderful happenings in her sheltered, pampered life had come to her through her beauty. She reached out an exquisite arm, switched on a light, and picking up a hand-mirror from a dressing-table, fell to studying her face. She was right. It was her chiefest asset. She forgot Stephen and fell asleep.

But in the morning her husband's voice issuing from his dressing-room across the hall, awakened her. She listened drowsily. Stephen, leaving the house the day before, had been met by a boy with a telegram. He had taken it, slipped it into his pocket, (he was just going to the mail-box) and had forgotten to deliver it until now, nearly twenty-four hours later. She could hear Stuart's storm of abuse—it was terrible, made up as it was of oaths and insults to the boy's ancestry. There was a moment's lull. Then she heard him again.

"If your brains are a fair sample of that black wench of a sister of yours—"

She sprang up then thrusting her arms as she ran into her pink dressing-gown. She got there just in time. Stephen, his face quivering, was standing looking straight into Wynne's smoldering eyes. In spite of herself, Amy was glad to see the boy's bearing. But he did not notice her.

"You devil!" he was saying. "You white-faced devil! I'll make you pay for that!" He raised his arm. Wynne did not blench.

With a scream she was between them. "Go, Stephen, go,—get out of the house. Where do you think you are? Don't you know you'll be hanged, lynched, tortured?" Her voice shrilled at him.

Wynne tried to thrust aside her arms that clung and twisted. But she held fast till the door slammed behind the fleeing boy.

"God! Let me by, Amy!"

"God, let me by, Amy!" As suddenly as she had clasped him she let him go, ran to the door, fastened it and threw the key out the window. He took her by the arm and shook her. "Are you mad? Didn't you hear him threaten me, me,—a nigger threaten me?" His voice broke with anger, "And you're letting him get away! Why, I'll get him. I'll set bloodhounds on him, I'll have every white man in this town after him! He'll be hanging so high by midnight—" he made for the other door, cursing, half-insane.

How, *how* could she keep him back! She hated her weak arms with their futile beauty! She sprang toward him. "Stuart, wait," she was breathless and sobbing. She said the first thing that came into her head. "Wait, Stuart, you cannot do this thing." She thought of Cornelius—suppose it had been he—"Stephen,—that boy,—he is my brother."

He turned on her. "What!" he said fiercely, then laughed a short laugh of disdain. "You are crazy," he said roughly, "My God, Amy! How can you even in jest associate yourself with these people? Don't you suppose I know a white girl when I see one? There's no use in telling a lie like that."

Well, there was no help for it. There was only one way. He had turned back for a moment, but she must keep him many moments—an hour. Stephen must get out of town.

She caught his arm again. "Yes," she told him, "I did lie. Stephen is not my brother, I never saw him before." The light of relief that crept into his eyes did not escape her, it only nerved her. "But I *am* colored," she ended.

Before he could stop her she had told him all about the tall white woman. "She took me to Mrs. Boldin's and gave me to her to keep. She would never have taken me to her if I had been white. If you lynch this boy, I'll let the world, your world, know that your wife is a colored woman."

He sat down like a man suddenly stricken old, his face ashen. "Tell me about it again," he commanded. And she obeyed, going mercilessly into every damning detail.

IV

Amazingly her beauty availed her nothing. If she had been an older woman, if she had had Zora's age and experience, she would have been able to gauge exactly her influence over Wynne. Though even then in similar circumstances she would have taken the risk and acted in just the same manner. But she was a little bewildered at her utter miscalculation.

She had thought he might not want his friends—his world by which he set such store—to know that she was colored, but she had not dreamed it could make any real difference to him. He had chosen her, poor and ignorant, out of a host of women, and had told her countless times of his love. To herself Amy Wynne was in comparison with Zora for instance, stupid and uninteresting. But his constant, unsolicited iterations had made her accept his idea.

She was just the same woman she told herself, she had not changed, she was still beautiful, still charming, still "different". Perhaps that very difference had its being in the fact of her mixed blood. She had been his wife—there were memories—she could not see how he could give her up. The suddenness of the divorce carried her off her feet. Dazedly she left him—though almost without a pang for she had only liked him. She had been perfectly honest about this, and he, although consumed by the fierceness of his emotion toward her, had gradually forced himself to be content, for at least she had never made him jealous.

She was to live in a small house of his in New York, up town in the 80's. Peter was in charge and there were a new maid and a cook. The servants, of course, knew of the separation, but nobody guessed why. She was living on a much smaller basis than the one to which she had become so accustomed in the last three years. But she was very comfortable. She felt, at any rate she manifested, no qualms at receiving alimony from Wynne. That was the way things happened, she supposed when she thought of it at all. Moreover, it seemed to her perfectly in keeping with Wynne's former attitude toward her; she did not see how he could do less. She expected people to be consistent. That was why she was so amazed that he in spite of his oft iterated love, could let her go. If she had felt half the love for him which he had professed for her, she would not have sent him away if he had been a leper.

"Why I'd stay with him," she told herself, "if he were one, even as I feel now."

She was lonely in New York. Perhaps it was the first time in her life that she had felt so. Zora had gone to Paris the first year of her marriage and had not come back.

The days dragged on emptily. One thing helped her. She had gone one day to the modiste from whom she had bought her trousseau. The woman remembered her perfectly—"The lady with the exquisite taste for colors—ah, madame, but you have the rare gift." Amy was grateful to be taken out of her thoughts. She bought one or two daring but altogether lovely creations and let fall a few suggestions:

"That brown frock, Madame,—you say it has been on your hands a long time? Yes? But no wonder. See, instead of that dead white you should have a shade of ivory, that white cheapens it." Deftly she caught up a bit of ivory satin and worked out her idea. Madame was ravished.

"But yes, Madame Ween is correct,—as always. Oh, what a pity that the Madame is so wealthy. If she were only a poor girl—Mlle. Antoine with the best eye for color in the place has just left, gone back to France to nurse her brother—this World War is of such a horror! If someone like Madame, now, could be found, to take the little Antoine's place!"

Some obscure impulse drove Amy to accept the half proposal: "Oh! I don't know, I have nothing to do just now. My husband is abroad." Wynne had left her with that impression. "I could contribute the money to the Red Cross or to charity."

The work was the best thing in the world for her. It kept her from becoming too introspective, though even then she did more serious, connected thinking than she had done in all the years of her varied life.

She missed Wynne definitely, chiefly as a guiding influence for she had rarely planned even her own amusements. Her dependence on him had been absolute. She used to picture him to herself as he was before the trouble—and his changing expressions as he looked at her, of amusement, interest, pride, a certain little teasing quality that used to come into his eyes, which always made her adopt her "spoiled child air", as he used to call it. It was the way he liked her best. Then last, there was that look he had given her the morning she had told him she was colored—it had depicted so many emotions, various and yet distinct. There were dismay, disbelief, coldness, a final aloofness.

There was another expression, too, that she thought of sometimes—the look on the face of Mr. Packard, Wynne's lawyer. She, herself, had attempted no defense.

"For God's sake why did you tell him, Mrs. Wynne?" Packard asked her. His curiosity got the better of him. "You couldn't have been in love with that yellow rascal," he blurted out. "She's too cold really, to love anybody," he told himself. "If you didn't care about the boy why should you have told?"

She defended herself feebly. "He looked so like little Cornelius Boldin," she replied vaguely, "and he couldn't help being colored." A clerk came in then and Packard said no more. But into his eyes had crept a certain reluctant respect. She remembered the look, but could not define it.

She was so sorry about the trouble now, she wished it had never happened. Still if she had it to repeat she would act in the same way again. "There was nothing else for me to do," she used to tell herself. But she missed Wynne unbelievably.

If it had not been for Peter, her life would have been almost that of a nun. But Peter, who read the papers and kept abreast of the times, constantly called her attention, with all due respect, to the meetings, the plays, the sights which she ought to attend or see. She was truly grateful to him. She was very kind to all three of the servants. They had the easiest "places" in New York, the maids used to tell their friends. As she never entertained, and frequently dined out, they had a great deal of time off.

She had been separated from Wynne for ten months before she began to make any definite plans for her future. Of course, she could not go on like this always. It came to her suddenly that probably she would go to Paris and live there—why or how she did not know. Only Zora was there and lately she had begun to think that her life was to be like Zora's. They had been amazingly parallel up to this time. Of course she would have to wait until after the war.

She sat musing about it one day in the big sitting-room which she had had fitted over into a luxurious studio. There was a sewing-room off to the side from which Peter used to wheel into the room waxen figures of all colorings and contours so that she could drape the various fabrics about them to be sure of the best results. But today she was working out a scheme for one of Madame's customers, who was of her own color and size and she was her own lay-figure. She sat in front of the huge pier glass, a wonderful soft yellow silk draped about her radiant loveliness.

"I could do some serious work in Paris," she said half aloud to herself. "I suppose if I really wanted to, I could be very successful along this line."

Somewhere downstairs an electric bell buzzed, at first softly, then after a slight pause, louder, and more insistently.

"If Madame sends me that lace today," she was thinking, idly, "I could finish this and start on the pink. I wonder why Peter doesn't answer the bell."

She remembered then that Peter had gone to New Rochelle on business and she had sent Ellen to Altman's to find a certain rare velvet and had allowed Mary to go with her. She would dine out, she told them, so they need not hurry. Evidently she was alone in the house.

Well she could answer the bell. She had done it often enough in the old days at Mrs. Boldin's. Of course it was the lace. She smiled a bit as she went down stairs thinking how surprised the delivery-boy would be to see her arrayed thus early in the afternoon. She hoped he wouldn't go. She could see him through the long, thick panels of glass in the vestibule and front door. He was just turning about as she opened the door.

This was no delivery-boy, this man whose gaze fell on her hungry and avid. This was Wynne. She stood for a second leaning against the door-jamb, a strange figure surely in the sharp November weather. Some leaves—brown, skeleton shapes—rose and swirled unnoticed about her head. A passing letter-carrier looked at them curiously. "

What are you doing answering the door?" Wynne asked her roughly. "Where is Peter? Go in, you'll catch cold."

She was glad to see him. She took him into the drawing room—a wonderful study in browns—and looked at him and looked at him.

"Well," he asked her, his voice eager in spite of the commonplace words, "are you glad to see me? Tell me what do you do with yourself."

She could not talk fast enough, her eyes clinging to his face. Once it struck her that he had changed in some indefinable way. Was it a slight coarsening of that refined aristocratic aspect? Even in her subconsciousness she denied it.

"This was no delivery-boy, this man"—

He had come back to her.

"So I design for Madame when I feel like it, and send the money to the Red Cross and wonder when you are coming back to me." For the first time in their acquaintanceship she was conscious deliberately of trying to attract, to hold him. She put on her spoiled child air which had once been so successful.

"It took you long enough to get here," she pouted. She was certain of him now. His mere presence assured her.

They sat silent a moment, the late November sun bathing her head in an austere glow of chilly gold. As she sat there in the big brown chair she was, in her yellow dress, like some mysterious emanation, some wraith-like aura developed from the tone of her surroundings.

He rose and came toward her, still silent. She grew nervous, and talked incessantly with sudden unusual gestures. "Oh, Stuart, let me give you tea. It's right there in the pantry off the dining-room. I can wheel the table in." She rose, a lovely creature in her yellow robe. He watched her intently.

"Wait," he bade her.

She paused almost on tiptoe, a dainty golden butterfly.

"You are coming back to live with me?" he asked her hoarsely.

For the first time in her life she loved him.

"Of course I am coming back," she told him softly. "Aren't you glad? Haven't you missed me? I didn't see how you could stay away. Oh! Stuart, what a wonderful ring!"

For he had slipped on her finger a heavy dull gold band, with an immense sapphire in an oval setting—a beautiful thing of Italian workmanship.

"It is so like you to remember," she told him gratefully. "I love colored stones." She admired it, turning it around and around on her slender finger. How silent he was, standing there watching her with his sombre yet eager gaze. It made her troubled, uneasy. She cast about for something to say.

"You can't think how I've improved since I saw you, Stuart. I've read all sorts of books—Oh! I'm learned," she smiled at him. "And Stuart," she went a little closer to him, twisting the button on his perfect coat, "I'm so sorry about it all,—about Stephen, that boy you know. I just couldn't help interfering. But when we're married again, if you'll just remember how it hurts me to have you so cross—"

He interrupted her. "I wasn't aware that I spoke of our marrying again," he told her, his voice steady, his blue eyes cold.

She thought he was teasing. "Why you just asked me to. You said 'aren't you coming back to live with me—'"

"Yes," he acquiesced, "I said just that—'to live with me'"

Still she didn't comprehend. "But what do you mean?" she asked bewildered.

"What do you suppose a man means," he returned deliberately, "when he asks a woman to live with him, but not to marry him?"

She sat down heavily in the brown chair, all glowing ivory and yellow against its sombre depths.

"Like the women in those awful novels?" she whispered. "Not like those women!—Oh Stuart! you don't mean it!" Her very heart was numb.

"But you must care a little—" she was amazed at her own depth of feeling. "Why I care—there are all those memories back of us—you must want me really—"

"I do want you", he told her tensely. "I want you damnably. But—well—I might as well out with it—A white man like me simply doesn't marry a colored woman. After all what difference need it make to you? We'll live abroad—you'll travel, have all the things you love. Many a white woman would envy you." He stretched out an eager hand.

She evaded it, holding herself aloof as though his touch were contaminating. Her movement angered him.

Like a rending veil suddenly the veneer of his high polish cracked and the man stood revealed.

"Oh, hell!" he snarled at her roughly. "Why don't you stop posing? What do you think you are anyway? Do you suppose I'd take you for my wife—what do you think can happen to you? What man of your own race could give you what you want? You don't suppose I am going to support you this way forever, do you? The court imposed no alimony. You've got to come to it sooner or later—you're bound to fall to some white man. What's the matter—I'm not rich enough?"

Her face flamed at that—"As though it were *that* that mattered!"

He gave her a deadly look. "Well, isn't it? Ah, my girl, you forget you told me you didn't love me when you married me. You sold yourself to me then. Haven't I reason to suppose you are waiting for a higher bidder?"

"She Lay Back Again on the Floor, Prone"

At these words something in her died forever, her youth, her illusions, her happy, happy blindness. She saw life leering mercilessly in her face. It seemed to her that she would give all her future to stamp out, to kill the contempt in his frosty insolent eyes. In a sudden rush of savagery she struck him, struck him across his hateful sneering mouth with the hand which wore his ring.

As *she* fell, reeling under the fearful impact of his brutal but involuntary blow, her mind caught at, registered two things. A little thin stream of blood was trickling across his chin. She had cut him with the ring, she realized with a certain savage satisfaction. And there was something else which she must remember, which she *would* remember if only she could fight her way out of this dreadful clinging blackness, which was bearing down upon her—closing her in.

When she came to she sat up holding her bruised, aching head in her palms, trying to recall what it was that had impressed her so.

Oh, yes, her very mind ached with the realization. She lay back again on the floor, prone, anything to relieve that intolerable pain. But her memory, her thoughts went on.

"Nigger," he had called her as she fell, "nigger, nigger," and again, "nigger."

"He despised me absolutely," she said to herself wonderingly, "because I was colored. And yet he wanted me."

V

Somehow she reached her room. Long after the servants had come in, she lay face downward across her bed, thinking. How she hated Wynne, how she hated herself! And for ten months she had been living off his money although in no way had she a claim on him. Her whole body burned with the shame of it.

In the morning she rang for Peter. She faced him, white and haggard, but if the man noticed her condition, he made no sign. He was, if possible, more imperturbable than ever.

"Peter," she told him, her eyes and voice very steady, "I am leaving this house today and shall never come back."

"Yes, Miss."

"I shall want you to see to the packing and storing of the goods and to send the keys and the receipts for the jewelry and valuables to Mr. Packard in Baltimore."

"Yes, Miss."

"And, Peter, I am very poor now and shall have no money besides what I can make for myself."

"Yes, Miss."

Would nothing surprise him, she wondered dully. She went on "I don't know whether you knew it or not, Peter, but I am colored, and hereafter I mean to live among my own people. Do you think you could find me a little house or a little cottage not too far from New York?"

He had a little place in New Rochelle, he told her, his manner altering not one whit, or better yet his sister had a four-room house in Orange, with a garden, if he remembered correctly. Yes, he was sure there was a garden. It would be just the thing for Mrs. Wynne.

She had four hundred dollars of her very own which she had earned by designing for Madame. She paid the maids a month in advance—they were to stay as long as Peter needed them. She, herself, went to a small hotel in Twenty-eighth Street, and here Peter came for her at the end of ten days, with the acknowledgement of the keys and receipts from Mr. Packard. Then he accompanied her to Orange and installed her in her new home.

"I wish I could afford to keep you, Peter," she said a little wistfully, "but I am very poor. I am heavily in debt and I must get that off my shoulders at once."

Mrs. Wynne was very kind, he was sure; he could think of no one with whom he would prefer to work. Furthermore, he often ran down from New Rochelle to see his sister; he would come in from time to time, and in the spring would plant the garden if she wished.

She hated to see him go, but she did not dwell long on that. Her only thought was to work and work and work and save until she could pay Wynne back. She had not lived very extravagantly during those ten months and Peter was a perfect manager—in spite of her remonstrances he had given her every month an account of his expenses. She had made arrangements with Madame to be her regular designer. The French woman guessing that more than whim was behind this move drove a very shrewd bargain, but even then the pay was excellent. With care, she told herself, she could be free within two years, three at most.

She lived a dull enough existence now, going to work steadily every morning and getting home late at night. Almost it was like those early days when she had first left Mrs. Boldin, except that now she had no high sense of adventure, no expectation of great things to come, which might buoy her up. She no longer thought of phases and the proper setting for her beauty. Once indeed catching sight of her face late one night in the mirror in her tiny work-room in Orange, she stopped and scanned herself, loathing what she saw there.

"You *thing*!" she said to the image in the glass, "if you hadn't been so vain, so shallow!" And she had struck herself violently again and again across the face until her head ached.

But such fits of passion were rare. She had a curious sense of freedom in these days, a feeling that at last her brain, her senses were liberated from some hateful clinging thralldom. Her thoughts were always busy. She used to go over that last scene with Wynne again and again trying to probe the inscrutable mystery which she felt was at the bottom of the affair. She groped her way toward a solution, but always something stopped her. Her impulse to strike, she realized, and his brutal rejoinder had been actuated by something more than mere sex antagonism, there was *race* antagonism there—two elements clashing. That much she could fathom. But that he despising her, hating her for not being white should yet desire her! It seemed to her that his attitude toward her—hate and yet desire, was the attitude in microcosm of the whole white world toward her own, toward that world to which those few possible strains of black blood so tenuously and yet so tenaciously linked her.

Once she got hold of a big thought. Perhaps there was some root, some racial distinction woven in with the stuff of which she was formed which made her persistently kind and unexacting. And perhaps in the same way this difference, helplessly, inevitably operated in making Wynne and his kind, cruel or at best indifferent. Her reading for Wynne reacted to her thought—she remembered the grating insolence of white exploiters in foreign lands, the wrecking of African villages, the destruction of homes in Tasmania. She couldn't imagine where Tasmania was, but wherever it was, it had been the realest thing in the world to its crude inhabitants.

Gradually she reached a decision. There were two divisions of people in the world—on the one hand insatiable desire for power; keenness, mentality; a vast and cruel pride. On the other there was ambition, it is true, but modified, a certain humble sweetness, too much inclination to trust, an unthinking, unswerving loyalty. All the advantages in the world accrued to the first division. But without bitterness she chose the second. She wanted to be colored, she hoped she was colored. She wished even that she did not have to take advantage of her appearance to earn her living. But that was to meet an end. After all she had contracted her debt with a white man, she would pay him with a white man's money.

The years slipped by—four of them. One day a letter came from Mr. Packard. Mrs. Wynne had sent him the last penny of the sum received from Mr. Wynne from February to November, 1914. Mr. Wynne had refused to touch the money, it was and would be indefinitely at Mrs. Wynne's disposal. She never even answered the letter. Instead she dismissed the whole incident,—Wynne and all,—from her mind and began to plan for her future. She was free, free! She had paid back her sorry debt with labor, money and anguish. From now on she could do as she pleased. Almost she caught herself saying "something is going to happen." But she checked herself, she hated her old attitude.

But something *was* happening. Insensibly from the moment she knew of her deliverance, her thoughts turned back to a stifled hidden longing, which had lain, it seemed to her, an eternity in her heart. Those days with Mrs. Boldin! At night,—on her way to New York,—in the workrooms,—her mind was busy with little intimate pictures of that happy, wholesome, unpretentious life. She could see Mrs. Boldin, clean and portly, in a lilac chambray dress, upbraiding her for some trifling, yet exasperating fault. And Mr. Boldin, immaculate and slender, with his noticeably polished air —how kind he had always been, she remembered. And lastly, Cornelius; Cornelius in a thousand attitudes and engaged in a thousand occupations, brown and near-sighted and sweet—devoted to his pretty sister, as he used to call her; Cornelius, who used to come to her as a baby as willingly as to his mother; Cornelius spelling out colored letters on his blocks, pointing to them stickily with a brown, perfect finger; Cornelius singing like an angel in his breathy, sexless voice and later murdering everything possible on his terrible cornet. How had she ever been able to leave them all and the dear shabbiness of that home! Nothing, she realized, in all these years had touched her inmost being, had penetrated to the core of her cold heart like the memories of those early, misty scenes.

One day she wrote a letter to Mrs. Boldin. She, the writer, Madame A. Wynne, had come across a young woman, Amy Kildare, who said that as a girl she had run away from home and now she would like to come back. But she was ashamed to write. Madame Wynne had questioned the girl closely and she was quite sure that this Miss Kildare had in no way incurred shame or disgrace. It had been some time since Madame Wynne had seen the girl but if Mrs. Boldin wished, she would try to find her again—perhaps Mrs. Boldin would like to get in touch with her. The letter ended on a tentative note.

The answer came at once.

My dear Madame Wynne:

My mother told me to write you this letter. She says even if Amy Kildare had done something terrible, she would want her to come home again. My father says so too. My mother says, please find her as soon as you can and tell her to come back. She still misses her. We all miss her. I was a little boy when she left, but though I am in the High School now and play in the school orchestra, I would rather see her than do anything I know. If you see her, be sure to tell her to come right away. My mother says thank you.

Yours respectfully,

CORNELIUS BOLDIN.

The letter came to the modiste's establishment in New York. Amy read it and went with it to Madame. "I have had wonderful news," she told her, "I must go away immediately, I can't come back—you may have these last two weeks for nothing." Madame, who had surmised long since the separation, looked curiously at flushed cheeks, and decided "Monsieur Ween" had returned. She gave her fatalistic shrug. All Americans were crazy.

"But, yes, Madame,—if you must go—absolument."

When she reached the ferry, Amy looked about her searchingly. "I hope I'm seeing you for the last time—I'm going home!" Oh, the unbelievable kindness! She had left them without a word and they still wanted her back!

Eventually she got to Orange and to the little house. She sent a message to Peter's sister and set about her packing. But first she sat down in the little house and looked about her. She would go home, home—how she loved the word, she would stay there a while, but always there was life, still beckoning. It would beckon forever she realized to her adventurousness. Afterwards she would set up an establishment of her own,—she reviewed possibilities—in a rich suburb, where white women would pay and pay for her expertness, caring nothing for realities, only for externals.

"As I myself used to care," she sighed. Her thoughts flashed on. "Then some day I'll work and help with colored people—the only ones who have really cared for and wanted me." Her eyes blurred.

She would never make any attempt to find out who or what she was. If she were white, there would always be people urging her to keep up the silliness of racial prestige. How she hated it all!

"Citizen of the world, that's what I'll be. And now I'll go home."

Peter's sister's little girl came over to be with the pretty lady whom she adored.

"You sit here, Angel, and watch me pack," Amy said, placing her in a little armchair. And the baby sat there in silent observation, one tiny leg crossed over the other, surely the quaintest, gravest bit of bronze, Amy thought, that ever lived.

"Miss Amy cried," the child told mother afterwards.

Perhaps Amy did cry, but if so she was unaware. Certainly she laughed more happily, more spontaneously than she had done for years. Once she got down on her knees in front of the little arm-chair and buried her face in the baby's tiny bosom.

"Oh Angel, Angel," she whispered, "do you suppose Cornelius still plays on that cornet?"

DOUBLE TROUBLE

ILLUSTRATED BY LAURA WHEELER

I

Angélique came walking delicately down Cedarwood Street. You could see by the way she advanced, a way which fell just short of dancing that she was feeling to the utmost the pleasant combination of her youth, the weather and the season. Angélique was seventeen, the day was perfect and the year was at the spring. Just before Cedarwood crosses Tenth, she stopped, her nice face crinkling with amusement, and untied and retied the ribbon which fastened her trim oxford. Before she had finished this ritual Malory Fordham turned the corner and asked rather sternly if he might not perform the task. "Allow me to tie it for you," he had said with unrelieved formality.

"Sure I'll allow you." Angélique was never shy with those whom she liked. She replaced the subtler arts of the coquette with a forthrightness which might have proved her undoing with another boy. But not with Malory Fordham. Shy, pensive, and enveloped by the aura of malaise which so mysteriously and perpetually hung over his household he found Angélique's manner a source both of attraction and wonder. To him she was a radiant, generous storehouse of light and warmth which constantly renewed his chilled young soul.

"We're in luck this afternoon," said Angélique resuming her happy gait. "Some-times I have to tie my shoes a dozen times. Once I took one shoe off and shook it and shook it, trying to get rid of make believe dust. I was glad you didn't turn up just then for I happened to look across the street and there was cousin Laurentine walking, you know that stiff poker-like way she goes—" Angélique bubbling with merriment imitated it—"I know she was disgusted seeing me like 'my son John, one shoe off and one shoe on'."

"It's a wonder she didn't take you home," said Malory, admiring her.

"Oh, no! Cousin Laurentine wouldn't be seen walking up the street with me! She doesn't like me. Funny isn't it? But you know what's funnier still Malory, not many folks around here do like me. Strange, don't you think, and me living all my life almost in this little place? I never knew what it was to be really liked before you came except for Aunt Sal. I say to myself lots of times: 'Well, anyway, Malory likes me,' and then I'm completely happy."

"I'm glad of that," Malory told her, flushing. He was darker than Angélique for his father and mother had both been brown-skinned mulattoes, with a trace of Indian on his mother's side. Angélique's mother, whom she rarely saw, was a mulatto, too, but a very light one, quite yellow, and though she could not remember her father, she had in her mind's eye a concept of him which made him only the least shade darker than her mother. He had to be darker, for Angélique always associated masculinity with a dark complexion. She did not like to see men fairer than their wives.

Malory dwelt for several moments on Angélique's last remark. You could see him patently turning the idea over and over. His high, rather narrow, forehead contracted, his almond, liquid eyes narrowed. His was a type which in any country but America would have commanded immediate and admiring attention. As it was even in Edendale he received many a spontaneous, if surreptitious, glance of approval.

He evolved an answer. "I don't know but you're right, Angélique. I think I must have been home six months before I met you, though I knew your name. I seem to have known your name a long time," he said musing slowly over some evasive idea. "But I never saw you, I guess, until that night when Evie Thompson's mother introduced us at Evie's party. I remember old Mrs. Rossiter seemed so queer. She said—"

"Yes, I know," Angélique interrupted, mimicking, "Oh, Miz Thompson, you didn't ever introduce them! That," concluded the girl with her usual forthrightness, "was because she wanted you to meet her Rosie—such a name Rosie Rossiter!—and have you dance attendance on her all evening!"

Fordham blushed again. "I don't know about that. Anyhow, what I was going to say was if I were you I wouldn't bother if the folks around here didn't like me. They don't like me either."

"No, I don't think they do very much. And yet it's different," Angélique explained puzzling out something. "They may not like you—probably because you've lived away from home so long—but they're willing to go with you. Now I think it's the other way around with me. They sort of like me, lots of the girls at times have liked me a great deal, new girls especially. But they shy away after a time. When Evie Thompson first came to this town she liked me better than she did any one else. I know she did. But after her mother gave that big party she acted different. She has never had me at a real party since and you know she entertains a lot —you're always there. Yet she's forever asking me over to her house when she hasn't company and then she's just as nice and her mother is always too sweet."

They were nearing the corner where they always parted. Cousin Laurentine did not allow Angélique to have beaux. "Perhaps they're jealous." Malory proposed as a last solution.

The girl's nice, round face clouded. She was not pretty but she bore about her an indefinable atmosphere of niceness, of freshness and innocence. "Jealous of the boys, you mean?" She bit her full red lip. "No, it's not that; none of the boys ever treats me very nicely, none of them ever has except you and Asshur Judson."

"Asshur Judson!" Malory echoed in some surprise. "You mean that tall, rough, farmer fellow? I'd have thought he'd be the last fellow in the world to know how to treat a nice girl like you."

"Mmh. He does, he did. You know the boys—most of them"—for the first time Fordham saw her shy, wistful—"when I say they're not nice I mean they are usually too nice. They try to kiss me, put their arms around me. Sometimes when I used to go skating, I'd have horrid things happen. They'd tease the other girls, too, but with me they're different. They act as though it didn't matter how they treated me. Maybe it's because my father's dead."

"Perhaps," Malory acquiesced doubtfully, but he was completely bewildered. "And you say Asshur Judson was polite?"

"I'd forgotten Asshur. You didn't know him well, I think; he came while you were still in Philadelphia and he went away after you came back. We'd been skating one day. I wasn't with anyone, just down there in the crowd, and I struck off all alone. Bye and bye who should come racing after me but Asshur. I looked back and saw him and went on harder than ever. Of course he caught up to me, and when he did he took me right in his arms and held me tight. I struggled and fought so that I know he understood I didn't like it, so he let me go. And then that hateful Harry Robbins came up and said: 'Don't you mind her, Jud, she's just pretending, she'll come around!'" Her voice shook for the shame of it.

"And then?" Malory prompted her fiercely.

"I heard Judson say just as mad, 'What the deuce you talking about, Robbins?'"

Malory failed to see any extraordinary exhibition of politeness in that.

"Oh, but afterwards! You know my Cousin Laurentine doesn't allow me to have company. Of course he didn't know that, and that night he came to the house. Cousin Laurentine let him in and I heard her say: 'Yes, Angélique is in but she doesn't have callers.' And he answered: 'But I must see her, Miss Fletcher, I must explain something.' His voice sounded all funny and different. So I came running down stairs and asked him what he wanted.

"It was all so queer, Malory. He came over to me past Cousin Laurentine standing at the door like a dragon and he took both my hands, sort of frightened me. He said: 'You kid, you decent little kid! Treat 'em all like you treated me this afternoon, and try to forgive me. If you see me a thousand times you'll never have to complain of me again.' And he went."

"Funny," was Malory's comment. "Didn't he say anything more?"

"No, just went and I've got to go. Got to memorize a lot of old Shakespeare for tomorrow. Silly stuff from Macbeth. 'Double, double, toil and trouble.' 'Bye Malory."

"Good-bye," he echoed, turning in the direction of his home where his mother and his three plain older sisters awaited him.

On his way he captured the idea which had earlier eluded him. He remembered speaking once, before he had met her, of Angélique Murray to his odd subdued household and of receiving a momentary impression of shock, of horror even, passing over his mother's face. He looked at his sisters and received the same impression. He looked at all four women again and saw—nothing—just nothing, utter blankness, out of which came the voice of Gracie, his hostile middle sister. "Good heavens, Malory! Don't tell me that you know that Angélique Murray. I won't have you meeting her. She is ordinary, her whole family is the last thing in ordinariness. Now mind if you meet her, you let her alone."

At the time he had acquiesced, deeming this one of the thousand queer phases of his household with which he was striving so hard to become reacquainted. He had been a very little boy when he had been taken so hurriedly to live in Philadelphia, but his memory had painted them all so different.

In spite of his sister's warning Angélique's brightness when he met her, her frankness, her merriment proved too much for him. She was like an unfamiliar but perfectly recognizable part of himself. Pretty soon he was fathoms deep in love. But because he was a boy of practically no ingenuities but mechanical ones he could hit on nothing better than walking home from school with her. She was the one picture in the daily book of his life and having seen her he retired home each day like Browning's lovers to think up a scheme which would enable him sometime to tear it out for himself.

THE TWO YOUNG WHITE LADIES WHO CAME TO SEE AUNT SAL AND LAURENTINE

Angélique, hastening on flying feet, hoped that Cousin Laurentine would be out when she reached home. She could manage Laurentine's mother, Aunt Sal, even when she was as late as she was today. But before she entered the house she realized that for tonight at least she would be free from her cousin's hateful and scornful espionage. For peeping through the window which gave from the front room on to the porch she was able to make out against the soft inner gloom the cameo-like features of the Misses Courtney, the two young white women who came so often to see Aunt Sal and Laurentine. They were ladies of indubitable breeding and refinement, but for all their culture and elegance they could not eclipse Laurentine whose eyes shone as serene, whose forehead rose as smooth and classical as did their own. The only difference lay in their coloring. The Misses Courtney's skin shone as white as alabaster; their eyes lay, blue cornflowers, in that lake of dazzling purity. But Laurentine was crimson and gold like the flesh of the mango, her eyes were dark emeralds. Her proud head glowed like an amber carving rising from the green perfection of her dress. She was a replica of the

Courtney sisters startlingly vivified. Angélique, on her way to the kitchen poising on noiseless feet in the outside hall, experienced anew her thrill at the shocking resemblance between the two white women and the colored one; a resemblance which missed completely the contribution of white Mrs. Courtney and black Aunt Sal, and took into account only the remarkable beauty of Ralph Courtney, the father of all three of these women.

Aunt Sal in the background of the picture was studying with her customary unwavering glance the three striking figures. The Misses Courtney had travelled in Europe, they spoke French fluently. But Laurentine had travelled in the West Indies and spoke Spanish. When the time came for the Misses Courtney to go, they would kiss Laurentine lightly on both cheeks, they would murmur: "Good-bye, Sister," and would trail off leaving behind them the unmistakable aura of their loyal, persistent, melancholic determination to atone for their father's ancient wrong. And Laurentine, beautiful, saffron creature, would rise and gaze after them, enveloped in a sombre evanescent triumph.

But afterwards!

Up in her room Angélique envisaged the reaction which inevitably befell her cousin after the departure of these visitors. For the next three weeks Laurentine would be more than ever hateful, proud, jealous, scornful, intractable. The older woman, the young girl shrewdly guessed, was jealous of her; jealous of her unblemished parentage, of her right to race pride, of her very youth, though her own age could not be more than twenty-eight. "Poor Cousin Laurentine," the child thought, "as though she could help her father's being white. Anything was liable to happen in those old slavery times. I must try to be nicer to her."

When later she opened the door to her cousin's tap her determination was put to a severe test, for Laurentine was in one of her nastiest moods. "Here is another one of those letters," she said bitingly, "from that young ruffian who pushed his way past me that night. If I had my way I'd burn up every one of them. I can't think how you manage to attract such associates. It will be the best thing in the world for all of us when your mother sends for you."

Angélique took Asshur's letter somewhat sullenly, though she knew the feeling which her cousin's outburst concealed. In that household of three women this young girl was the only one who could be said to receive mail. Even hers was, until very lately, almost negligible—a note or two from a proudly travelling schoolmate, some directions for making candy from Evie Thompson or from the girl who at that moment was espousing her inexplicable cause, a card or so from a boy and now this constant stream of letters from Asshur Judson. As she opened these last or sat down to answer them in the shaded green glow of the dining-room, she had seen Cousin Laurentine's face pale with envy under the saffron satin of her skin.

Laurentine received letters and cards from the Misses Courtney when they were abroad—a few bills—she made rather a practice of having charge accounts—and an occasional note from the white summer transient expressing the writer's pleasure with "that last dress you made me". Once the young divinity student who, while the pastor was on his vacation, took over the services of the African Methodist Episcopal Church, sent her a post card from Niagara Falls. Laurentine exhibited a strange negligence with regard to this card; it was always to be found in the litter of the sewing-table. "Oh," she would say casually to the customer whom she was fitting, "that's a card from Mr. Deaver who substituted here last summer. Yes, he does seem to be a fine young man."

Angélique did not at once open Asshur's letter. She had too many lessons to get. Besides she knew what it would contain, his constant and unvarying injunction "to be good, to be decent" coupled with an account of his latest success in some branch of scientific agriculture; he was an enthusiastic farmer. She liked to hear from him, but she wished his interests were broader. Laying the letter aside unregretfully she fell to memorizing the witches' speech in Macbeth and then in her little English Handbook under the chapter on "The Drama—Greek Tragedy," she made a brief but interested foray among the peculiarities of the ancient stage. Reading of Greek masks, buskins and "unities" she forgot all about Asshur's letter until as usual Aunt Sal put her fine dark head in the door and told her in mild but unanswerable tones that it was "most nigh bedtime".

She jumped up then and began to undress. But first she read the letter. Just as she thought it began like all his former letters and would probably end the same. No, here was something different. Asshur had written: "My father says I'm making great headway, and so does Mr. Ellis, the man on whose farm I'm experimenting. Next year I'll be twenty-one and father's going to let me work a small farm he owns right up here in northern New Jersey. But first I'm coming for you. Only you must keep good and straight like you were when I first met you. You darn spunky little kid. Mind, you be good, you be decent. I'm sure coming for you."

It was a queer love-letter. "So you'll come for me," said Angélique to her image in the glass. She shook out her short, black, rather wiry hair till it misted like a cloud about her childishly round face. "How do you know I'll go with you? I may find someone I like ten times better." Dimpling and smiling she imitated Malory's formality: "May I tie your shoe for you?"

All night long she dreamed she was chasing Malory Fordham. Was it a game? If so why did he so doggedly elude her? Then when, laughing, she had overtaken him, why did he turn on her with round gaping mouth and horrid staring eyes that transformed him into a Greek tragic mask? Through open, livid lips came whistling strange words, terrible phrases whose import at first she could not grasp. When she did she threw her arm across her face with a fearful cry and fell back convulsed and shuddering into the arms of a dark, muffled figure whose features she fought vainly to discover.

II

Edendale, like many another Jersey town, as well as all Gaul, was divided into three parts. In one section, the prettiest from a natural point of view, lived Italians, Polacks and Hungarians who had drifted in as laborers. In another section, elegant and cultivated, dwelt a wealthy and leisure class of whites, men of affairs, commuters, having big business interests in Philadelphia, Trenton, Newark and even New York. Occupying the traditional middle ground were Jews, small tradesmen, country lawyers and a large group of colored people ranging in profession from Phil Baltimore, successful ash-contractor to the equally successful physician, Dr.

Thompson. This last group was rather closely connected with the wealthy white group, having in far preceding generations, dwelt with them as slaves or more recently as house-servants. Sometimes as in the case of Aunt Sal Fletcher and the Courtneys, who following the Civil War, had drifted into Jersey from Delaware, they had served in both capacities.

Malory and Angélique came to know the foreign quarters well. Here on the old Hopewell Road beginning nowhere and going nowhither they were surest of escaping the eye of a too vigilant colored townsman as well as that of the occasional white customer for whom the girl's cousin sewed. Malory was in no danger from a possibility like this last for the Fordhams on the maternal side had been small but independent householders for nearly a century. Even now Mrs. Fordham lived on a small income which came partly from her father's legacy, partly from the sale of produce from a really good truck-farm. Her husband had showed a tendency to dissipate this income but he had died before he had crippled it too sorely. Malory was determined to have more money when he grew older, money which he would obtain by his own methods. He never meant to ask his family for any-thing. The thought of a possible controversy with the invincible Gracie turned him sick.

He would be an engineer, how or where he did not know. But there would be plenty of money for him and Angélique. Already all his dreams included Angélique. He had not told her but he loved her fervently with an ardor excelling ordinary passion, for his included gratitude, a rapt consciousness of the miracle which daily one wrought for him in the business of living. She was so vivid, so joyous, so generous, so much what he would wish to be that almost it was as though she were his very self. Every day he warmed his hands at that fire which she alone could create for him.

He it was who fought so keenly against the clandestine nature of their meetings. Not so Angélique. This child so soon, so tragically to be transformed into a woman, was still a romantic, dreaming girl. Half the joy of this new experience lay in its secrecy. This was fun, great fun, to run counter to imperious, unhappy Laurentine, to know that while her cousin endured the condescending visit of the son of the ash-contractor in the hope that some day, some how she might receive the son of the colored physician, she herself was the eagerly and respectfully chosen of the son of the first colored family in the county. This was nectar and ambrosia, their taste enhanced by secrecy.

But Malory hated it. He had not told his family about the girl because clearly for some fool reason they were prejudiced against her, and as for Angélique's family—no males allowed. Hence this impasse. But he wanted like many another fond lover to acquaint others with his treasure, to show off not only this unparalleled gem, but himself too. For in her presence he himself shone, he became witty, his shyness vanished. The Methodist Sunday School picnic was to be held the first week in June. His sisters never went; proud Laurentine would not think of attending. He told Angélique that he would take her.

"Wonderful!" she breathed. She had a white dress with red ribbons.

They met on that memorable day, rather late. Laurentine could not keep Angélique from attending the picnic, but she could make her late; she could make her feel the exquisite torture which envelops a young girl who has to enter alone and unattended the presence of a crowd of watchful acquaintances. Angélique inwardly unperturbed,—she knew Malory would wait for her forever,—outwardly greatly chafing, enjoyed her cousin's barely concealed satisfaction at her pretended discomfiture. With a blithe indifference she went from task to task, from chore to chore. "Greek tragedy," she whispered gaily into the ear of Marcus, an adored black kitten.

Malory did not mind her lateness. Indeed he was glad of it. So much the more conspicuous their entrance to the grounds. As it chanced, practically the whole party was in or around the large pavilion grouped there to receive instructions from Mrs. Evie Thompson who had charge of the picnic. A great church-worker, Mrs. Evie. When the two arrived the place was in an uproar, Mrs. Evie, balanced perilously on a stool tried to out talk the noise. Presently she realized that her voice was unnecessarily loud, the sea of black, yellow, and of white faces had ebbed into quiet but not because of her. Malory just outside the wide entrance, in the act of helping Angélique up the rustic steps caught that same fleeting shadow of horror and dismay, that shadow which he had marked on the faces of his household, rippling like a wave over the faces of the crowd, touching for a second Mrs. Thompson's face and vanishing. Appalled, bewildered, he stood still.

Mrs. Thompson rushed to them. "You just happened to mest Angélique, Malory? You—you didn't bring her?" Her voice was low but anxious.

"Of course I brought her," he replied testily. What possessed these staring people? "Why shouldn't I bring her?"

"Why not indeed?" soothed Mrs. Thompson. She herself came from a "best family" in some nearby big city. "It's such luck that's all. I was wishing for Angélique. She's such a help at a time like this, so skilful. I want her to help me cut sandwiches."

Malory, rather sulkily accepting this, allowed his guest to be spirited away to exercise this skill. The crowd drawing a vast, multi-throated breath dispersed. Mrs. Thompson was anything but skilful herself. In the course of the afternoon she cut her assistant's hand. "I don't anticipate any infection," she remarked, peering at the small wound with an oddly unrepentant air, "but you'd better come home with me and let Doctor dress it. Sorry I can't invite you too Malory, but there's hardly room in the buggy for four. Evie and I are both fat."

Malory passed a night of angry sleeplessness. "I don't know what to think of these people," he told Angélique when they met the next day. "Do you know what I want you to do? You come home with me now and meet my mother and sisters. When they get to know you, they'll like you too and I know they can make these others step around." It was the first time he had betrayed any consciousness of the Fordham social standing.

Angélique, nothing loth, agreed with him. She too had thought Mrs. Thompson extraordinary the day before, but she had not seen as Malory had that strange shadowy expression of horror. And in any case would have had no former memory to emphasize it.

The two moved joyously up the tree-lined street, Malory experiencing his usual happy reaction to Angélique's buoyancy. Nothing would ever completely destroy her gay equanimity he thought, feeling his troubled young spirit relax. There was no one like her he knew. His people, even Gracie, must love her. He was living at this time in the last years of the nineties and so was given to much reading of Tennyson. Angélique made him think of the Miller's daughter, who had "grown so dear, so dear". What of life and youth and cheerfulness would she not introduce into his drab household, musty with old memories, inexplicably tainted with the dessication of some ancient imperishable grief!

At the corner of the street he took her arm. They would march into the house bravely and he would say, "Mother this is Angélique whom I love. I want you to love her too; you will when you know her." He perceived as he opened the gate that Angélique was nervous, frightened. Timidity was in her such an unusual thing that he felt a new wave of tenderness rising within him. On the porch just before he touched the knob of the screen door he laid his hand on hers.

"Don't be frightened," he murmured.

"Look," she returned faintly.

He spun about and saw pressed against the window-pane a face, the small, brown face of his sister Gracie. In the background above her shoulder hovered the head of the oldest girl Reba, her body so completely hidden behind Gracie's that for a second, it seemed to him fantastically, her head swung suspended in space. But only for a second did he think this, so immediately was his attention drawn, riveted to the look of horror, of hatred, of pity which was frozen, seared on the faces of his sisters.

"For God's sake, what is it?" he cried.

Gracie's hands made a slight outward movement toward Angélique, a warding off motion of faintness and disgust such as one might make involuntarily towards a snake.

"I'm going in; come Angélique," the boy said in exasperation. "Has the whole world gone crazy?"

Before he could open the door Reba appeared, that expression still on her face, like a fine veil blurring out her features. Would it remain there forever he wondered.

"You can't bring her in Malory, you mustn't."

"Why mustn't I? What are you talking about?" Strange oaths rose to his lips. "What's the matter with her?" He started to pull the door from his sister's grasp when Gracie came, pushed the door open and stepped out on the porch beside him.

"Oh Malory you must send her away! Come in and I'll tell you." She burst into tears.

Gracie his tyrant, his arch-enemy weeping! That startled him far more than that inexplicable look. The foundations of the world were tottering. He turned to his trembling companion. "Go home, Angel," he bade her tenderly. "Meet me tomorrow and we'll fix all this up." He watched her waver down the porch-steps then turned to his sisters:

"Now girls?"

Together they got him into the house and told him. ...

III

Angélique said to herself, "I'll ask Aunt Sal,—Cousin Laurentine,—but what could they know about it? No I'll wait for Malory. Can I have the leprosy I wonder?" She went home, stripped and peered a long time in the mirror at her delicate, yellow body.

Next afternoon near the corner of Cedarwood and Tenth she untied and retied her shoes twenty times. Malory did not come. She shook out bushels of imaginary dust. He had not come, was never coming.

At the end of an hour she went to the corner and peered down Tenth Street. Yes—no—yes it was he coming slowly, slowly down the steps of the Boys' High School. Perhaps he was sick; when he saw her, he would be better. ... He did not look in her direction; without so much as turning his head he came down the steps and started due west. Cedarwood Street lay east.

Without a second's hesitation she followed him. He was turning now out of Tenth north on Wheaton Avenue. After all you could go this way to the old Hopewell Road. Perhaps he had meant for her to meet him there. A block behind him, she saw him turn from Wheaton into the narrow footpath that later broadened into Hopewell Road. Yes, that was what he meant. She began to run then feeling something vaguely familiar about the act. On Hopewell Road she gained on him, called his name, "Malory, oh Malory" He turned around an instant, shading his eyes from the golden June sunlight to make sure and spinning back began to run, almost to leap, away from her.

"MALORY," SHE BESOUGHT PITIFULLY

Bewildered, horrified, she plodded behind, leaving little clouds of white dust spiraling up after her footsteps. As she ran she realized that he was fleeing from her in earnest; this was no game, no lover's playfulness.

He tripped over a tree-root, fell, reeled to his feet and, breathless, found her upon him. She knew that this was her dream but even so she was unprepared for the face he turned upon her, a face with horrid, staring eyes, with awful gaping lips, the face of a Greek tragic mask!

She came close to him. "Malory," she besought pitifully. Her hand moved out to touch his arm.

"Don't come near me!" His breath came whistling from his ghastly lips. "Don't touch me!" He broke into terrible weeping. "You're my sister,—my sister!" He raised tragic arms to the careless sky. "Oh God how could you! I loved her, I wanted to marry her,—and she's my sister!"

To proud Laurentine sitting in haughty dejection in the littered sewing-room, fingering a dog-eared postcard from Niagara Falls came the not unwelcome vision of her stricken cousin swaying, stumbling toward her.

"Laurentine, tell me! I saw Malory, Malory Fordham; he says,—he says I'm his sister. How can that be? Oh Laurentine be kind to me, tell me it isn't true!" She would have thrown herself about the older woman's neck.

Inflexible arms held her off, pushed her down. "So you've found it out have you? You sailing about me with your pitying ways and your highty-tighty manner. Sorry for Cousin Laurentine,—weren't you?—because her father was white and her mother wasn't married to him. But my mother couldn't help it. She had been a slave until she became a woman and she carried a slave's traditions into freedom.

"But her sister, your mother," the low, hating voice went on, "whom my mother had shielded and guarded, to whom she held up herself and me —me—" she struck her proud breast—"as horrible examples,—your mother betrayed Mrs. Fordham, a woman of her own race who had been kind to her, and ran away with her husband." She spurned the grovelling girl with a disdainful foot. "Stop snivelling. Did you ever see me cry? No and you never will."

Angélique asked irrelevantly: "Why do you hate me so? I should think you'd pity me."

Her cousin fingered the postcard. "Look at me." She rose in her trailing red dress. "Young, beautiful, educated,—and nobody wants me, nobody who is anybody will have me. The ash-contractor's son offers,—not asks, —to marry me. Mr. Deaver," she looked long at the postcard, "liked me, wrote me,—once,—"

"Why did he stop?" Angélique asked in all innocence. Laurentine flashed on her. "Because of you. You little fool, because of you! Must I say it again? Because my mother was the victim of slavery. People looked at me when I was a little girl; they used to say: 'Her mother couldn't help it, and she is beautiful.' They would have forgotten all about it. Oh why did your mother have to bring you home to us! Now they see you and they say: 'What! And her mother too! A colored man this time. Broke up a home. No excuse for that. Bad blood there. Best leave them

alone.'"

She looked at Angélique with a furious, mounting hatred. "Well you'll know all about it too. Wait a few years longer. You'll never be as beautiful as I, but you'll be pretty. And you'll sit and watch the years go by, and dread to look in your mirror for fear of what you'll find there. And at night you'll curse God,—but pshaw you won't,—" she broke off scornfully, "you'll only cry—"

Angélique crept up to her room to contemplate a future like Laurentine's.

Hours later Aunt Sal come in, her inscrutable dark face showing a blurred patch against the grey of the room. In her hand something gleamed whitely.

"Thought you might want yore letter," she said in her emotionless, husky voice.

Her letter, her letter from Asshur! Her letter that would reiterate: "Be a good kid and I'll come for you. ..."

She seized it and fell half-fainting in the old woman's arms. "Oh Asshur I'll be good, I'll be good! Oh Aunt Sal, help me, keep me. ..."

PERSONAL ESSAYS

TRACING SHADOWS

Few things, it seems to me, offer so much ground for speculation as the psychology of the proverb. I like to pause and consider the series of striking incidents and co-incidences which have finally moved some man to utter the remark which afterwards becomes the trite aphorism of all the ages.

"Coming events cast their shadows before." How often has that thought come to me during this tempestuous year which has elapsed since we entered the train at Calais last June. Opposite us in the little compartment sat a woman, black-haired, restless, curious and polyglot. She was friendly too and within five minutes had told us of her parentage—Spanish and English it was—of her Italian husband who strolled persistently through the corridor unheeding her advice to sit down and keep quiet. It would be so like him, she told us in her Italian-Spanish-French to step off the train and be left behind; "he is of such a carelessness that Giovanni." And then all in the same breath she added, "you have heard of the terrible news? No? But ladies it is so awful. The Archduke and Archduchess of Austria have been attacked and killed by a Serbian." She knew her history, that lady, and I learned more of the fateful record of the ill-starred Hapsburgs then, than I had ever heard in my life. Also I gained for the first time a faint concept of the immense importance which the doings of one European state holds for another—a concept destined, indeed, to become most emphatic within the next six weeks.

It is not far from Calais to Paris, at least it was not in those days. At six o'clock we had reached our haven. Contrasting the court-yard of the Care des Nord, its taxis and bustling crowds with that quite other panic-stricken scene of seven weeks later, it seems as though I must have had a bad dream. But then! No one, I am sure, is ever homesick in Paris. We had been wretchedly so in London but Paris—with its lights and people and thronged streets, its motor-busses and its inimitable atmosphere—Paris was for us and we were for Paris! Forgotten were the murdered Archduke and his poor Duchess. Elated with the thought that our Stratford-atte-Bowe French had been understood not only by a polyglot lady of no fixed nationality, but also by a Parisian taxicab driver we were whirled through a network of marvelous streets, past "les Italiens" down the Avenue de l'Opera, through Fourth of September Street to the Hotel de la Neva in little Rue Monsigny. I haggled for a few delicious seconds over the pourboire, (for had not the black-haired lady of Calais warned us against tipping too freely?) the proprietor "R. Deck" led us courteously within, we shot upwards in a tiny elevator (ascenseur) and presently found ourselves in an immaculate room. Our personal siege of Paris had begun. And at dinner Madame Deck, looking at us with her limpid gray eyes, (red with weeping now, I suppose, like so many other French women's) said, "You ladies have doubtless heard that the Archduke and Archduchess of Austria have been killed. Quel dommage! We hope there will be no trouble!"

I have neither time nor space to tell at length of what we saw in those intervening days. Nor can I explain the charm of Paris. I do not know in what it consisted. Perhaps it was in the sight of the students dancing in the streets at the fourteenth of July fete, or in the merry, childish throng that flocked to Versailles the Sunday after to see the fireworks. Sometimes the Artist of our little group sat with Our Lady of Lei sure in the Luxembourg Gardens and sketched those happy, happy children of the bourgeoisie. Sometimes all five of us, the Musician, Our Lady of

Leisure, the Artist, the other Student and myself went off on long expeditions. Once a charming Scotch girl and the Artist and the Lady and I went to the Bois on a picnic whose piece de resistance was a large bottle of white wine, the gift of the Scotch girl's father. And everywhere was charm and light and the joy of living.

I wonder if great joy ever bursts on one with the same unexpectedness as does disaster. It seems to me that it does not. Perhaps that is because most of us strive more or less consciously toward happiness and so each is well aware of the various steps he takes to ward what will spell for him the magic condition. Certainly we did not notice the shadows which coming events were casting before. And yet as we look back I can trace them so distinctly that I cannot conceive how I missed their import. On that last Tuesday in July one of the American Art students—we had moved into the "Quarter" to be near the school which I attended—who lived in our house remarked on the excitement prevailing in the streets that day. But were not French people not ably excitable? On Wednesday as the other Student and I walked home from school across the "Boule St. Miche" and through the Luxembourg Gardens, he told me that Austria had declared war on Servia. It seemed ridiculous to us then—a big nation like Austria against little Servia. It was too absurd! As for France getting into the war! Still that evening at dinner I asked the proprietor of the little restaurant on the Boulevard du Montparnasse—Jonathan Podd we used to call him—what he thought of that possibility. His pale face turned paler as he assured me, "But no, mademoiselle, it is absurd!" Poor Jonathan Podd! By the following Wednesday he had gone. I wonder if he has ever seen since his little "Hotel" and his wife of the beautiful rosy cheeks and soft black hair.

On Thursday the Lady and I cashed our last draft preparatory to leaving for Switzerland in a few days. We were offered and stupidly took the whole sum—between two and three hundred dollars—in paper money of large denomination. Gold and silver coin was already beginning to run to shelter. That afternoon we went to Versailles again, and either the other Student or the Musician, I've forgotten which, stopped to get the tickets for all five. He came back with a little puzzled frown. "Isn't it funny?" he said. "I offered them a fifty-franc note (ten dollars) and they said they couldn't change it. Who ever heard of a railway station where they couldn't change ten dollars?" That did strike us as queer, but we found the proper coin among us and went on to Versailles just the same. Right in front of the palace gate I discovered that I had lost a twenty-franc gold piece (four dollars). That, in view of what was to follow, was indeed a shadow.

Friday, the thirty-first, was not momentous except that we went to Chantilly and spilt fully half the sandwiches on the ground as we sat in the little grove at the entrance to the "course." That might have been a shadow had not those two gallant chevaliers, the other Student and the Musician, declared that they had not as yet eaten their full peck of dirt and were not averse to completing it now.

But Saturday, the first of August! That was the day the church bells rang all over the city—for mobilization they told us gravely. I don't believe I ever knew the verb "to mobilize" until August, 1914. By Sunday morning the event whose shadows had been cast a month before had come. Germany had declared war on France.

Those days that followed, those restless throbbing days! For us, of course, they spelt confusion—our Lady and I had practically no money that was not paper, and that might just as well have been the actual rags of which paper is made. I had just lost four dollars in gold—precious gold—at Versailles and the Artist was little better off than we. There were hasty visits to the Consulate and Embassy with highly unsatisfactory interviews. There were baffling announcements to the effect that if one wanted to leave Paris he must do so in twenty-four hours having first obtained a permit of departure. If one wanted to stay in Paris he must obtain a permit to remain there. There was a heart-breaking waiting in line at the prefecture only to find out after six weary hours that one had gone to the prefect in the wrong ward. There was the wearying, nerve-racking strain to be undergone all over again the next day.

But what were we and our petty troubles compared with a nation's agony? I am grown-up now. I have lived in two or three large cities. I have seen and known many people. I have seen and felt sorrow and grief and pain. But I have never seen anything—never dreamed of anything like the nightmare of sorrow and grief and pain which fell last August, on Paris—on France. I hope that God will be good enough never to let me see its like again. Sorrow and Grief and Pain, I said, mark you. Dismay? Yes. Anger—of course. But fear—never!

In all those days of awfulness and anguish of women weeping in the streets, of men walking along with reddened eyes, of sweethearts strolling "once more for the last time" through the Tuileries and the rapidly deserted Luxembourg Garden, of whole families sending their men away in anguished silence—never did I see any sign of fear. But oh! the sense of disaster, of impending fatality.

As a young and impressionable child I read once, I remember, of a very wealthy man who had gained his riches by grinding the face of the poor throughout the earth. One night he was awakened from sleep by a fearful sound. It was the concentrated wail of all the people he had wronged the world over. I have never forgotten the awfulness of that idea. Picture to yourself some such concentration of misery and pain and suffering of all the people in France and you know something of the pall which hung over the nation last summer. It was a veritable twilight of the Gods.

Two weeks elapsed before we could leave Paris. In that time my brain must, I think, have become a camera. I have but to close my eyes to see some scenes. There was the young woman to whom I talked one afternoon in those pathetic Luxembourg Gardens. Her home had been in Belfort. Her father and uncle had fought in 1870 and had apparently talked ever since of the great revanche. "Mademoiselle," she said, "I have heard of war all my life,—and now, mon dieu, it is here."

It was Sunday afternoon, and we were sitting listlessly about waiting, waiting. Somebody tapped and in came Eugene. Eugene, the valet de chambre, the courteous, the indefatigable, the ever cheerful. When the war broke out Eugene a "brave" of twenty-four, I suppose, had smiled. "But, of course, mademoiselle, I shall be going to the war." He threw out his chest under his blue apron, his eyes shone. But this was a different Eugene, fine in his blue coat and the senseless red trousers of the French private. He had come to tell us good-bye. "I must go to-night," he told us brokenly, "it is necessary. I shall never come back." His eyes were wet—we were frankly in tears. "Oh Eugene, must you go at once," I said, "and what about your fiancee?" He had told me of his girl. "I cannot even see her," he told us. I must go at once." And we, with our hands full of that foolish paper money, could give him only a couple of francs for his tabac, —for we were almost penniless.

Poor, brave Eugene! And poorer, braver Victorine! She was the maid of all work (la bonne a tous faire). One had only to see her look at Eugene to know where her heart was. And what mattered it if he did like somebody else? Was the somebody else not in another city, and was not she Victorine in the same house with him and could she not see him every day? But now—"I shall never see him again mademoiselle," she told me the next day, "and he did not even leave me his picture." And she threw her apron over her poor, quivering face and ran upstairs.

Everywhere were soldiers—privates in blue three-quarter length coats, the lower corners in front, buttoned back with a brass button to the side, —their legs in red trousers, a perfect target for some German bullet,—soldiers in light-blue coats, officers, I suppose, with medals strung across them. Horsemen brave in scarlet and shining helmets, a tuft of horsehair streaming over their shoulders; mounted policemen in sober, darkblue. Through the streets they marched and rode, faces set and grave without a single strain of music. And nothing added to the solemnity of the occasion as much as that.

One of those soldiers I like to remember—the one who rode with us from Paris to Amiens. A serious, earnest man he was even for those serious, earnest times, some sort of officer I think. He eyed us in grave silence for a while but presently he began to talk. His was a fine patriotism; no regrets, no ifs, no buts, no foolish boastings. But one knew that he had only one thing to offer to La Patrie—and that was his best always. He took his bayonet out and let us hold and finger it, and explained in great detail the terrible consequences of the wound which it inflicted. And finally, when some chance remark led him to realize that we had left Paris without breakfast, he delved deep into his knapsack and produced some thick milk chocolate which he pressed upon us. I have never tasted anything so delicious. It was a perfect godsend, for although in June it had taken us only two hours to go from Amiens to Paris, it took us in August, six hours to go from Paris to Amiens. We asked him timidly to allow us the privilege of giving him some money for du tabac,—we wanted, as Americans, to show him this slight token of our good will. But he refused us gravely. He had done only what a gentleman should do, he assured us earnestly, and had in our gratitude and sympathy received more than a gentleman's reward.

Two other scenes remain with me—one of which, after all, I never saw, but rather heard. Back of where we stopped in little rue Brea, lived a girl and I should judge, her mother. Their voices were so happy. Every day, I think, this must have taken place. The girl, who played the piano very indifferently, used to begin to practice. She would go through her exercises listlessly, then break off and begin a little folk-song which she played indifferently well too, but which she evidently loved. Perhaps her mother meant to scold her but the folk-song was obviously too much for her, and she would leave her occupation and lean, I fancy, over the girl's shoulder and sing the little ditty along with her. Sometimes a young man's voice would join in too, and they would sing it over and over again. I think it happened every day for five weeks. It was a simple but hauntingly, sweet melody. Eugene used to whistle it around the corridors and I meant to ask him its name and how to obtain it, but I forgot. When we returned to America, Our Lady of Leisure and I found out that we still remembered the melody and we have set a phrase of it at the head of the article. But after the war broke out, we never heard either it or, indeed, any other sound issue from the house back of us. Poor mother and poor youth, and poor, sweet jeune fille!

And now I come to what, to me, was the most important, because most indicative incident of all. We had gone late that Wednesday afternoon to our little restaurant. It was deserted except for us and to us presently came poor Jonathan Podd's pretty wife. She had been crying, poor thing, and when she saw us, she started afresh. "My husband has gone, ladies," she told us, polite even in her great anguish, "he had to go today." She served us—but how could we eat? And then she sat down in the back of the place and picked up a basket of green peas and began to shell them. At intervals she would choke down a sob and murmur, "oh mon dieu, mon dieu!"—but she kept on shelling peas. Work must go on, life must be lived, she could not falter even though her husband had gone to an accursed war and the world for her lay in ruins.

Well that was France, that is France. Because of her delicate sensibilities, when her tragic hour came, she wept careless that all the world could see and know, but falter, shrink, hesitate,—never! Were peas to be shelled there were her women choking back sobs, and working on with eyes too blinded by tears to see. Were guns to be shouldered. There was always Eugene.

And so it seems to me that here is one of the rare occasions where one dares quote the proverb before the happening of the event. And just as we have looked backwards from the war and traced out the shadows which presaged it, just so we may follow up these new indications,—the attitude of Eugene and the wife of Jonathan Podd made manifold many millions of times—to the next event which is surely coming—a new and evermore wonderful France.

Dear France! When, finally we left Boulogne, and the cliffs of—oh I hope I err when I say the cliffs of that "perfidious Albion" were rising white before us, I looked back in the direction of France and wished I knew how to voice the feeling which my heart held for her. But the benizon remained unspoken, for I had no words. Since then Gabriele D'Annunzio has done it for me, and what he has said, is I know, the quintessence of the sentiment of all her worshippers:

> "France, sweet France, Love of the world,
> France, France, what a world without thee."

NOSTALGIA

On those rare mornings when I have a moment to spare I go into the little fruit shop on Seventh Avenue and buy a hard, sweet, red apple and a small rusty orange. The foreign proprietor knows me now and greets me with as much eagerness as though I were about to buy out all his stock. There are bunches of ruddy grapes hanging up on a piece of twine; the precious life-juice is dying out of them and they are becoming shrunken purple masses. They fascinate me.

"Will those grapes become raisins?" I asked him finally.

"They would if they were left there long enough, but that is not the usual way. As a rule they gather the grapes and dip them into hot water in which potash"—he looks in his pocket dictionary for the word—"has been boiled. Then they hang them up, to cure in the sun."

I like the subject. "Where is all this done. In California, in Italy?"

"In Greece," he corrects me, his tongue lingering with love on the word. My interest switches.

"And you are Greek?" He is short and squat and one eyelid droops. I have to readjust my views, a misleading composite taken from the Hermes of Praxiteles and the storied heroes of Homer.

"I am a Greek," he says slowly, and momentarily is transformed. "I like this country," he anticipates me, "but in Greece—ah! it is so different." He sighs.

Somehow I get a vision—Greece and the Acropolis many templed; olive trees, sunny vineyards, garlanded messengers running Pheidippides-wise with an ardor that takes the arduousness out of their labor.

I ask him where he lives; in Larissa, in Arcadia, in Elis?

His answer is a classic phrase.

"I live in the islands of the sea." He names his particular island, but neither Xenophon or Lysias trains one's ears too well for modern Greek. I am loath to ask him again, afraid to break the spell.

He sighs and sweeps his drooping gaze about the store. "In the summer I shall sell my stock, and if I am lucky, *if I am lucky*, I shall go back." He does not mean if he is lucky at his sale, but if the gods favor him, if the fates are kind, his will be the ecstatic privilege of returning.

"But it is hard to make a living in Europe," I remind him and hate my materialism.

"It does not cost much to live, though," he counters. "With only a little one can get along." He clutches at his manners. "I like America, you know, but in Greece—ah—I cannot tell you what I mean. In Greece it is so different."

I go thoughtfully through the muddy ways to the little cobbler shop on Twelfth Street and sit down to have my boots cleaned.

My handsome Italian bootblack leaves his cobbling and begins on my shoes.

"Well, how you like this weather?" he asks in a loud voice, which makes me think somehow that he is talking to keep up courage.

I like the weather well enough, being used to the flurry of snow and the grey winter days of our eastern coast.

"In Italy, where I come from, it would be so sunny and the skies would be blue." He pauses in his work with a shoe brush in each hand. But he makes a romantically wistful figure for all that.

He is homesick, too, poor fellow. But he has not learned the lesson of the older Greek—that contentment is best—is the only thing. He is young, he thinks he must make money which will bring success, happiness.

He was in the war, and tells me about it with wide, extravagant gestures. He has a fine head and deep, dark eyes that glow. I am sorry for him. He seems so caught, so trapped by life, so deserving of a better fate. Incurable sentimentalist though I am, I am still unable to cast a halo about the profession of cobbler and bootblack.

"I shall never, never forget the 19th of September and the 6th of October. I fought in the Argonne on those days in 1918. I never thought to come back alive." We both forget my boots. Let them dry or go uncleaned altogether. One does not hear an iliad at first hand every day.

Even in his enthusiasm he is mournful.

"You did not fight with the Italians then?"

He shakes his head sadly. "No, I am American now. I go fight with Americans. Some day I go back to Italy maybe, but not now."

"You don't like Italy?"

Not like it! He looks at me speechless for a second. How can one ask such a question? "It is so hard to make a living in Italy," he tells me simply. "When I make plenty of money, then I go back and stay forever."

I look around the mean shop, with its iron stove in the center, which keeps only itself warm; I glance at the pile of ugly, wrinkled shoes over which he spends his hours, and reflect how hard indeed must it be for the poor in Italy, if in spite of soft skies and blue seas, he can force himself to live thus under the shadow of the 6th Avenue "L."

I always give him double his price,—I did it timorously at first, but he took it with a quiet gratitude. He must have needed it—for that spirit would never accept alms. Rather his manner says, "You can afford to give it; I can afford to take it. We are both helping each other."

He sees me to the door with a magnificent bow. All his movements are spontaneous, at once awkward and graceful like those of a child or a faun.

At the door—"Well, good-day. You come in again soon? Yes?"

His tragic eyes follow me out into the drab weather, pass beyond me, across the Alps, to Italy!

Nostalgia—homesickness! All languages must have the word. It is as universal a phenomenon as that of possessing a mother. The Greek stem *nostos* means a returning home, and *algos* means pain. A pain for returning home! How vivid and keen that is! The French speak of *la nostalgie*, personifying it. The Germans have *Heimweh*—home-woe. That pulls at the heart-strings. I asked my Italian for the word in his tongue—"*amor di patria*, love of fatherland," he said. I don't know whether or not the single word exists, but love of fatherland is certainly nostalgia's cause.

It is of all pangs the least endurable. For it there is only one cure. Sometimes it arises from the lack of material things,—familiar scenes, skies, flowers, food. Sometimes it arises from the lack of things of the spirit, a difference in ideals. That is very hard to bear.

Across from the College Settlement, at Fourth and Christian Streets, in Philadelphia, lives Rachel, aged twelve. She comes over once to seek her flyaway younger sister, Bessie, and remains to visit with me. There was never a quicker recognition of kindred spirits.

Rachel should have lived in the great days of France. Hers would have been a marvelous salon, out-rivaling the *Hôtel de Rambouillet*. All, all things in this world are to be talked about, not quickly, but slowly, relishfully, with a choosing of fit words, a probing into inner meanings and much reflection between topics. Such is Rachel's code.

She does not come over to the settlement regularly because she goes to school every morning—even through the long, hot August which we are now enduring—to study Hebrew—and she aged twelve! She pronounces her name Rachel for me with a combination of aspirate and guttural, which I am powerless to reproduce either with tongue or with pen.

"My father says we should all be well educated," she explains. "Education, he thinks, is a great thing. He is a Zionist—if you know what that is," she ends doubtfully.

I do know, I hasten to inform her quickly. I would not for anything show ignorance in the presence of this grave young personage. She has very white skin of the tint we call pearly, the dark seeing eyes of the sybil and a noble head.

"And your father expects to go to Jerusalem?"

"Yes, he has a farm there and some day he is going to sell out here and go to Jerusalem to stay forever."

This strikes me as foolhardy. "Has he ever been to Jerusalem."

"No, my father is from Roumania and so is my mother. We were born in America, but all my father's and mother's people are Roumanian Jews. But my father,"—she says in her grave voice with its precise accent, "my father says, 'Here or in Roumania it is all the same,—no place for a Jew. For a Jew, living in a Christian country is like being a stranger in some-one's else house. You are never at home; you always feel you are not wanted. But Jerusalem,' he says, 'that is ours, we can do as we please; nothing that we do shall be odd. The other people will be the strangers.'"

I am no longer doubtful.

"And your mother and all of you will go? You want to go?"

Rachel shakes her curly head—so youthful by contrast with her serious manner.

"My mother does not want to go. She says, 'Why should we go to Jerusalem? What will we do? If we make money, what will we have to spend it on?' She says she will stay here and open a store."

"But your father will not go off without her and you. He won't want to go by himself."

"My mother wouldn't, but my father would. My mother," intones Rachel, "says to my father, 'A father's heart is not like a mother's. You could go off and leave your children or take them to a strange land. I am their mother. I must stay with them and keep them where is comfort.'"

I should like to be present at these dignified, aphoristic disputes.

The father comes to the gate one day to inquire after Bessie,—Bessie, who will never know the meaning of homesickness. Wherever Bessie is, there will be home. She is six and short and charming, with merry blue eyes that glance quickly squirrel-wise, a cherubic head and a ready tongue. Nothing of the introspective about Bessie.

But the father! He has plainly come to see me, for we stand facing each other in the narrow gateway, and he makes no attempt to look beyond. Perhaps Rachel has told him of her new confidante. He is small and slight in a nondescript, baggy grey suit and a little cap. He wears the thin, wispy, circular beard of the Semitic, around the chin and half way up the jaw-bones. And his eyes see visions.

Abruptly he is satisfied and bids me good-day.

"It is unfortunate that his wife is such a materialist," I think.

The very next day Rachel corrects me.

"My mother," she begins apropos of nothing, "does not want to go to Jerusalem, but she would like to go back to Roumania. 'Ah, Roumania!' she says, 'what difference would it make if we had nothing to live on if we were only back there!' My mother," reflects Rachel aloud, as though realizing this for the first time, "always cries when she speaks about Roumania."

So she is homesick, too! I am sorry for her, but I am sorrier for him. She has at least had some time that which she craves so unceasingly. Her ideal is static, it is just a matter of ships and trains and money. But his ideal—who shall say that he will find—even in Jerusalem—freedom for the Jew? And yet it must be somewhere, he reasons, with his keen Jewish mind, else all the presaging great movements of the world—the French Revolution, the Great War—have been lies.

His is a homesickness of the spirit!

On a rainy, blowy night in Philadelphia my doorbell rings and I usher in the colored boy whom I used to see at the Art School. He left his classes very hurriedly to go to France, and this is the first time I have seen him since his return. He towers above me in the magnificent and yet vaguely unfamiliar khaki of a second lieutenant. The magnificence and the unfamiliarity alike, he explains to me later, are due to its French cut.

"I wanted my mother to see how I *could* look," he grins boyishly.

She certainly must have approved of his looks, as must any one else who sees him, for he stretches up, up, well over six feet, with a marvelous development of brawn and muscle.

I get him into the warm dining room and proffer him tea and other comforts. He eats—cavernously. "It's so wonderful to get back to civilian fare," he tells me.

"And home," I add.

His young face undergoes a startling change. "Home?" he echoes, "where is it? Do you know, I never knew what home was until I went to France? There in the midst of all those strange people, and the awful food and the foreign jabber, I felt myself less homesick than I have ever felt in my life—yes, than I feel this minute.

"Home," he rushes on, his words tumbling over each other in his eagerness, "I don't know how to define it. Is it where one is surrounded by the sights and sounds to which he's been used all his life? Or is it where mentally and spiritually he is recognized and taken for what he is? What is home?"

I think of a line in an old hymn—

"Oh, what is that country and where can it be?"

"I didn't realize it while I was away," he goes on somberly. "I used to put up with the army prejudice, along with the dirt and noise and fighting as part of the general show. And when something too bad happened, I'd lay it to a few individual prejudiced Americans in command. But I used to think, 'Well, anyway, it'll be all right when I get back.'"

He laughs shortly. "I've been home one month. The second week I went to Arkansas to take my uncle a message and some things his boy had sent him. He died over there,"—this very simply—"and I knew uncle wanted to hear all about it. ... I hadn't been in town ten hours before white boys,—boys for whom my cousin had died,—stopped me on the street with, 'Nigger, you can't stay around here in that uniform. Take it off or git!' I wanted to put up a fight, but my uncle couldn't see it. He spirited me away that night, wouldn't hear to my staying.

"And there are hosts of others—Gosh! to think of it—born and bred in America—and I'm homesick for France!"

He gets up. "I'm leaving just as soon as I can."

"You don't mean to tell me," I say in amazement, "that you're actually going back—and to stay?"

"And my mother and—a girl I know,"—he softens a little. "Oh, I can find plenty to do. You know I wanted to be an architect. Where'd I get a chance at that here? America is all right, only not for us. French people and their customs are different, but they know how to make a man feel he's a man, all right."

A hasty handclasp and he is plunging out into the bitter night.

It is from the spiritual nostalgia that the American Negro suffers most. He has been away so long from that mysterious fatherland of his that like all the other descendants of voluntary and involuntary immigrants of the seventeenth century,—Puritan, pioneer, adventurer, indentured servant,—he feels himself American. The past is too far past for him to have memories. Very, very rarely does he have a backward reaching bond, be it never so tenuous.

Mr. Du Bois indeed in his "Darkwater" tells in a striking passage in that striking book of a Bantu ancestress who hugged her knees and swayed and sang:

"Do bana coba—gene me, gene me!

Ben d'nuli, ben d'le—"

Who knows what scene of Afric sands and Afric freedom those words may have conjured up? How the bleakness of New England and the harshness of captivity must have fostered her homesickness!

In the main, the American Negro is without ties and the traditions that throw back. Instead, he has built unconsciously from his childhood a dream-country, and yet surely no dream country since it is founded on that document which most realize and sets forth the primal and unchanging needs of man—the Constitution of the United States.

Where the Greek dreams of his statues, he dreams of Justice; where the Italian yearns for his opera, he yearns for Opportunity; and where the Jewish visionary longs for freedom of sect, he cries out for an escape from Peonage.

As a child in his readers, he learns of great principles in the Declaration of Independence, in Fourth of July speeches, in extracts from Daniel Webster, in Mr. Lincoln's Gettysburg address.

He grows up and finds them—not here—just beyond, always beyond; in a country where all things are possible he has found exactly what ought not to be possible.

He keeps on longing for these principles with an aching, voiceless longing; with Chateaubriand's "Exile" he sighs:

"Their memory makes me sorry every day."

Is he mocking himself? The cold fear strikes him that perhaps there is no such country. The Greek—if he is lucky—will return to his island of the sea. He knows it is there. The Italian will *go back* to Italy sometime. At least the Jews *have* lived in Jerusalem. But the black American is something entirely new under the sun. Shall he ever realize the land where he would be?

"For thee, oh dear, dear country,

Mine eyes their vigil keep!"

That second lieutenant is doomed to know homesickness of both body and spirit. In France he will want the comforts of America; in America, he cries out for the rights of man which he knew in France.

A nostalgia of body and soul—there is nothing harder to bear.

SUNDAY AFTERNOON

To the visual-minded all impressions come in a series of little pictures. To myself, for instance, who can remember only by opening and closing camera-fashion a little inward shutter—all my life stretches backward in a group of single detached visions. In one of these, more vivid than the rest, I see myself a small gloomy child sitting dejectedly in my little red chair.

"What on earth is the matter?" asks a merry older sister. "What are you crying about?"

And I answer as my tears break forth without reserve, "Today seems like Sunday."

Always Sunday afternoon has made me sad. But it is a sweet sadness. It must have been connected at first, I think, with the inhibitions which Sunday in a very conservative, not to say very religious household, placed, upon the small child. I might not sing songs, I might not play, I didn't know how to write letters, it was wrong to read even fairy-tales. I could not spend pennies for candy. And the stretch between dinner and supper—one had old-fashioned suppers in those days, cold beef and prunes!—the distance between the two meals was interminable. Of course, there was Sunday School, but even that, which I truly liked, did not remove the feeling of restraint and forlornness which can come to a child on a dreary enforced holiday.

There was a Dante's Inferno in our house, I remember, illustrated by Doré. That was permissible reading. I could not understand the text, but how I pored over those gloomy pictures. And there was a Family Bible, too, a fat leather-bound volume printed on stained brown paper with the old-fashioned s and with an Apocrypha. I was used to the Old Testament, so used that its queer outlandish names did not seem queer to me. But how I thrilled to those strange new titles, *Esdras*, *Holafernes*, *Judith*, *Susanna!* Their exotic quality remains with me still.

I can almost taste the atmosphere of those far-off times. Myself, with my precious book upstairs on the bed or on the floor, flat on my stomach, heels up, chin propped in my hands, and about me even on bright afternoons an indefinable sense of something gloomy, dark and melancholy. From below floated the sound of my sisters' voices chatting with the casual Sunday Caller. Sometimes there was a burst of laughter, then presently the welcome clatter of tea-things. After supper there was music—hymns, played on the organ; in summer-time a gathering on the front steps, a general sense of good-fellowship and reunion in which I joined gladly. But before that time in the late afternoon, gray or golden as the season might bring,—for me nothing but aloofness and sadness.

Later I came to cherish that period, came to sense its possibilities. I think I recognized it as the period of my greatest mental clarity. I seemed to be penetrated at such times with a startling realization of the value of things. Perhaps in this very realization lay sadness. At first I put, hardheadedly enough, this clarity, this mental keenness to a practical purpose. In college I found that notes reread on Sunday afternoon stayed by me, translations came more accurately and yet more delicately But I was never satisfied. Underneath was a longing to be doing something else, to be being, if I may say so, a totally different creature. The something else was always just beyond my ken. I tried to translate it into action. If the chapel-bell rang I thought I wanted to go to chapel. But when I went I found I was disappointed. If I strolled along the path which meant so much to me during my busy week, I found it meant nothing on Sunday. And always there was that sense of having missed something. My precious Sunday afternoon had gone and I still had not fathomed its meaning.

Lately I have found out what it means to me now. The realization came in France, as I sailed—not on a Sunday afternoon—on one of those ridiculous little boats which ply up and down the Seine. I was sitting idly apart not talking, not listening even to the other members of our little party, when over me came creeping that familiar Sunday feeling. It was not merely the mental clarity, for that comes too on a lonely railroad journey and is due, I think, to a certain sense of physical detachment, but there was the old familiar sweet, sweet wholly satisfactory melancholy.

"Doesn't to-day seem like Sunday?" I asked my astonished companions."

It was in the blessed period before the war. Paris was still gay, the Seine was alive with small craft, its banks crowded with fishing gentry. Nothing could be farther from the old-fashioned American idea of Sunday. But my heart knew.

Let me see if I can put it into words. It is so nebulous, yet to me so real. I found I wanted nothing at those times but the Sunday afternoon itself (or the time that seemed like that) and the sense of completeness which it brings. And perhaps it is this sense of wanting nothing beyond, which as a child made me so sad. The feeling which comes to me then is its own excuse for being. Am I *triste*? I would not be merry. Do I pine? The desire is sweeter than its satisfaction. Do I dream? No dream that has ever come true is sweeter than those dreams on Sunday afternoons when I brood "on no great things done, but great things undone". In that sweet do-nothingness of attitude, mental and physical—everything takes on an exquisitely true value which is immediately recognizable without any extra adjustment. It is as though the picture, the view had been focussed just for my special degree of short-sightedness. My heart and my mind are without strain.

Just to think, then, becomes for me a joy on Sunday afternoons. At first, I used to save problems for that happy season, but I soon learned better. Now I relax and let the thoughts come to me. How the difficulties resolve themselves. Sometimes it is a really vexing material puzzle, sometimes it is a bit of verse, sometimes a situation in a play, an abstruse expression that baffles. If my mind reverts to the puzzle and I pick up the book I find myself poring over it with the same intense concentration with which in my childhood I pored over Doré or the Apocrypha. And like then there is no sense of effort.

If I fail to give an idea of the ineffable satisfaction which now I gain on these beatific afternoons, I have written vainly. Everything is perfect. I would not hurry or hold back one moment. I am like the gourmet caressing his wine against his palate, yet letting it go, knowing he must not try too long to hold its flavor. Whatever I elect to do in those so brief hours is in itself an end. Sometimes I take out letters knowing that I shall not answer them then. Or I may hunt feverishly among a heap of papers for a half finished poem. Perhaps I add a line or two, but oftenest my content is complete in having unearthed it. Rarely I get out my accounts, but I believe I have never checked them up.

What I like most is to sit or lie motionless and let the stray sound or the glimpsing of a picture bring me my thought. Church-bells on Sunday afternoon throw me into an ecstasy of pleasant feeling—my college days drift back to me, and later wanderings in Quebec,—priests toiling laboriously up those tortuous streets to some house of prayer.

The church-bells remind me, too, of a French story, so exquisite, so complete as to give one the sensation of assisting at the creation, the unfolding of a rare and perfect thing, a flower, a poem, an utterly melodious song. In the story the church-bells take wing on good Friday and fly to Rome, whence they return on Easter Sunday. If one can spy them in their stately flight above the clouds, one's dearest wish will be granted. It seems to me nothing could be more exquisite, more French. I know I have found no conceit so restful, so pillow-y for the overstrung mind.

There is a picture on my wall that intrigues me repeatedly. On Sunday afternoons I let its atmosphere envelop me, absorb me. It is Rossetti's "Dorigen of Brittany", a picture none too well-known in this country.

The artist is illustrating a line from that much older artist, Chaucer. The picture, a soft platinotype, is full of all those harmonious unlikely things which the pre-Raphaelites insisted on grouping—there is a pipe-organ, a winding stair, a missal book, and a lady her arms outflung in despair to the sea just glimpsed through the open casement.

"Is there not any ship on all the seas that will bring back to me my dearest lord?"

Such is her plaint. Poor, mute, sad lady! If she only knew, she might be content. She has me to suffer vicariously for her. I picture the Breton fishing village, the angry sea, the tortured hearts of waiting women and my heart breaks with her own.

Sundays in winter are sweetest. The soft, gray closing-in of the afternoons between November and March induces a pleasant, restful melancholy. Whereas the hot glare of summer Sundays, in the park, say, the gay dresses, the motors, the boats, the very vividness of the trees—all these things cry for happiness. And if one because of some lack either within or without cannot achieve it one suffers more by contrast. On the other hand Sunday afternoon in a warm room with many books and few pictures and fewer or no people! Without, a hint of snow or the lowering that means rain; within, a flash of fire on the walls! Pain becomes a pleasure.

Of late I have spent my afternoons reading. Always the same thing. The *Apology for Socrates and Crito*—I cannot get away from it. And every perusal brings me fresh pleasure, a new and growing satisfaction. Here, in this old man's sublime and fearless attitude toward death, lies, it seems to me, the world's greatest brief for personal honor and probity. See him a man of seventy, with only a short while left. Surely he might be accounted blameless if accepting Crito's offer, he left the thankless Athenians and spent his few remaining years in Thessaly. But, listen to his noble simplicity,—

"Not life, Crito," he says, "but living well is to be prized."

Other men perhaps have said the same thing, but for me these words are unspeakably touching from the lips of this grand old pagan. All that he says is so sane, so balanced, so possible to weave into the stuff of one's own life.

"In all times of peril," he continues, "there are ways of escape if one will submit to any baseness. Athenians, it is not so hard to shun death, but hard indeed to shun evil, for that runs more swiftly than death. I, you see, an old man and slow of gait, have been overtaken by the slower runner."

I find myself transported with his dignity and sonorousness.

The years pass and I with them have passed from the childhood of that melancholy little girl to the not unmixed pleasures of womanhood. Through the bye-gone days gleam to my visual mind those precious afternoons like little emerald islands in a vast watery expanse. Not a joy but has been made fuller, not a grief but has been calmed and soothed by the influence of those few hours which induce,

That sweet mood when pleasant thoughts
Bring sad thought to the mind.

The warfare of modern living beats and seethes about my consciousness as it does about the rest of the world. But on Sundays, I lose some of its overwhelming impingement. Through the long years to come I see stretching before me a vista of blessed oases, little havens whither my tired heart and mind shall, not vainly, seek repose. And this vision is not the least of my indebtedness to Sunday afternoon.

WHEN CHRISTMAS COMES

What strange power does the sense of smell wield over the gates of memory? This morning, stepping into the cold, I sniffed a rush of snow-laden air that carried me back down the slope of yesterdays to a scene which I had completely forgotten. It was Christmas Eve in Philadelphia —a proper Christmas Eve I remember, for outside the snow was falling softly, thickly, warmly, but within, the house was bright with Christmas spirit, a light in every window. It was so like a conventional Christmas card and I had so often wanted to experience the sensation of the weary traveller who struggles up the snow-laden road toward the glowing house, that yielding to the persuasions of a daring older sister, I ventured with her out into the street.

"Around the block" we ran, hatless and coatless, I believe, right in the face of the soft, warm, blurry snow. Oh, what a sense of adventure and what a feeling of joy and relief was ours when we got back to the sheltering house with its bright, dry rooms! We slipped in unnoticed except by another sister who, perturbed by our vagrancy, had kept a discreet watch. She didn't tell on us—there's no fun in invoking punishment on Christmas Eve. Instead she produced unexpectedly a store of warm, soft ginger cookies fresh from the batch then in process of manufacture in the kitchen. Never ask me how she procured them.

Childhood, my own childhood certainly, photographs many such sharp detached pictures destined to return to one in later years with a wistful, indefinable poignancy. Sometimes does it not seem that that childish life was the real, the permanent, thing, and that these grown-up days of flashing, restless achievement are hardly worth the long preparation which one in his teens and first twenties endures?

My first trip to France did not so completely, so lengthily absorb me as did the preparations which we children used to make for Christmas in that old square-roomed house in Philadelphia. I think we must have begun in November. There was always a tree and so every year "Christmas things" had to be made for it. Such a buying of such gorgeous materials! Glazed paper in marvelous colors, a soft, deep, yet bright, blue; a warm, passionate red; a heart-of-the-melon pink. And because of the glaze on the paper all these colors possessed a curious, palpable quality; you could feel the color as well as see it. As a child I thought there must even be some way of absorbing it, especially that wonderful heartening, inspiring red. Besides the glazed paper there were sheets of thinner gold and silver with a slightly embossed figure; smaller sheets of gold stars, yards of tinsel, white, creamy paper lace, dozens of glass icicles and, of course, paper-dolls.

We made endless chains of the glowing colors and dressed the paper-dolls in tissue paper and lace. I had forgotten the possibilities of the tissue paper from which we contrived a round sort of pompoms which were fancifully designated "snow-balls" and another round but differently shaped paper mass called "water lilies." You made the snow-balls by twisting the ends of a circular piece of paper which had been slit down the edges into finger-width petals. Sometimes you gave too sharp a twist and the end of the petal came off. The water-lilies achieved their perfection with the aid of the head of the ordinary hat-pin. I cannot describe how this was done—the process is at once too simple and too intricate. Snowballs and water lilies alike were of all colors, but that discrepancy never troubled us.

Have I ever enjoyed anything since, I wonder, with the same intensity and the same sharp anticipation with which I enjoyed the Christmas season? There was a big square darkish room up in the top of the house where we children used to foregather and plan and plan for the holidays.

Actually we had a little chant, *"Oh, won't it be joyous when Christmas comes! Oh, won't it be joyous when Christmas comes!"* You said it with a stress on the second "won't" which converted it into a pleasing and irresistible rhythm which in itself created that joy you were so happily anticipating. I think that whatever modicum of unselfishness or generosity I now possess dates back from those days. For it was then I learned the sheer joy of giving. We children gave, I fear, with too little discrimination. Neckties and whisk-brooms for my father, and handkerchiefs for my mother. We could not think of anything else to give but we wanted to give. Gloves sometimes, perhaps, but that strained our tiny purses. It took two donors to provide one pair of gloves. My poor parents! They must have groaned at the inevitability of those unvarying presents.

Christmas Day when one is grown up is apt to be stodgy, too redolent of the taste of "the day after the night before." But the Christmas Day of my childhood was an endless round of new joys. First the stockings, always an orange in the toe and then quantities and quantities of nuts and raisins and candies. I can see us children now rushing from our rooms down the dark, chilly stairs, and exclaiming: "Oh, he did come, he did come! That's my stocking, see I pinned my name on it." There was a bright, thin tinkle of happy girlish voices and at intervals the discontented undertones of my brothers complaining because their stockings were not as long as ours. My mother always hung up my father's socks for them, I don't know why.

Some grown-ups complain because they were fooled by the Santa Claus myth, but I have always been glad of it. Surely there can be no lovelier way of starting one's own private little output of faith, hope and charity than this conception of an embodied spirit of kindness, riding red-faced and jolly throughout the land. I was a big girl, almost ready for high school, before I began seriously to consider the extreme inadequacy of any chimney-place of ours for a possible Santa Claus. Gradually I drifted into the truth of the matter, but I have never regretted for a moment the sweet foolery of my first belief.

But to return to the joy of Christmas Day. After the discovery of the bursting stockings, there were the presents to be examined. We received dolls for which I did not care very much—useful presents, a dress, a coat, a cap and books. And that was my reason for liking Christmas! After the long, wonderful dinner with its plethora of turkey and cranberry sauce, there was the long, dark, cozy afternoon to be spent in reading. There were always relatives at Christmas dinner and these and the rest of the household, it is to be presumed, disported themselves according to their various tastes. My own idea of indoor sport was to lie on the floor midway between the gorgeous tree and the glowing fire and to bury my head, my mind, my whole being, in some fairy tale or strange romance. I had been taught to read when I was just past babyhood. Small wonder then that at eight some one either with or without (I've never been able to determine which) a sense of humor, gave me a copy of "Don Quixote," the hardest nut which my childish mind ever tried to crack. I missed the broad farce and the sly wit which I am told penetrates that book. Doubtless I was a humorless child and took the story seriously. I know to this day I can never become interested in it.

What I did read with interest, with amazement, with resentment, with tears, was "Uncle Tom's Cabin." It lay a greyish brown volume, thick-leaved and large lettered on the kidney-shaped table in our parlor. It belonged to my grandmother whom I had never seen. But I had seen the book, and though the sight of most books was a challenge to me, I had never glanced inside this one. But on a certain Christmas Day, weary of Rose-Red and Snow-White, I happened to peep within those prim covers. They had to pry the book from my unwilling fingers. At the end of three or four days I had read it all, every word of it. I do not think I have ever opened it since but the story remains part of my permanent mental furnishings.

Supper on Christmas Night was negligible. Probably there would not have been any had it not been for "the boys." But the time after supper stands out bright and sharp before me. Those relatives and older ones probably went on later to their own devices, but we children grouped ourselves together and sang hymns, beautiful, immortal, glorious hymns: "Holy Night"; "Joy to the World"; "Oh! Come All Ye Faithful" (my father's favorite); and "Hark! The Herald Angels Sing." How sweet and solemn and altogether lovely that time was. I have felt the rush of wings.

...

My mother's favorite song was one which had nothing to do with the Christmas tide but which embodied the spirit of life in the house. It began "When the woods are dim and dreary," and asked "What then?" The refrain ran as I well remember:

> *"Ah! In spite of wind and weather,*
> *Round the fireside gleaming bright,*
> *We will sing old songs together,*
> *All the merry winter night!"*

Can anything more exquisitely define home? Ah, lovely little pictures of the heart borne back to me across the years on a breath of snow-laden air! They recreate for me each season of the Nativity the spirit of a Merry Christmas.

YARROW REVISITED

This is not the Paris of my student days nor even the Paris of the second Pan-African Congress held three years ago. I seem to glimpse in the memories of those visits an enchanted city of gay streets, blue skies, of romantically historic monuments, a playground, a court of justice of the world. Every one was possessed of a fine courtesy; attendants were kind and generous, though even then a little too conscious, for an American, of the possibility of tips; there was a delicious sense of *laisser-aller*.

Perhaps the difference lies in the season. I have never been here before so late in the year. One speaks of France and its golden weather as though that condition were perpetual. It is only October but the skies are drab, the days are grey and every twenty-four hours rain falls, steady, penetrating, soaking. The boulevards are still full, even crowded, but with Frenchmen now, not tourists; one meets with as much courtesy here, no more, no less, than anywhere else. In brief, life in Paris is life the civilized world over. But there is one exception.

I am glad to have had those golden memories of former visits. Yet I am glad to be here now in this workaday season. "Life as she is—" that is what I want to know even if it is different to the verge of disappointment from preconceived notions. Truth is best. Yet dreams are fine stuff too. In the last of those three poems of Wordsworth on Yarrow,—Yarrow Unvisited, Visited, Revisited, there are, I remember, these words:

"The visions of the past
Sustain the heart in feeling
Life as she is—"

It is precisely because of those visions that I am eager to know life, French life "as she is".

Just as the weather is by no means always golden and gay, so French living is not always a thing of joy and laughter.

I am not living in the vicinity of the gay, wide boulevards. I lived there three years ago. Nor am I in the "Quartier Latin", the famous student quarter; I spent some months there when I was a student. From both of these former environments my faulty impressions. No this time I am installed high up in a small, quiet hotel on a rather narrow but busy side-street, though still near the "quarter". It is far, far from the *Boulevard des Italiens*. But it is right in the heart of a teeming business and residential section.

I love comfort, I love ease. I do not consider laziness a crime. I hate to move. Yet so determined am I to see "Life as she is" that with as much joy as reluctance have I mapped out this plan:

Two weeks in a cheap pension. (Already over, thank God!)

A month in this small, comfortable hotel. (There is a fire-place in my room.)

A month in a "good" French family.

A month in a first-class pension.

After that such travel as my remaining means and time may permit.

\The pension held, as I suspect all cheap boarding houses do, the elements of unspeakable dreariness. It was a large house built inevitably of stone, set romantically, I thought at first, far, far back in a court-yard to which one gained access by one of those thick, slowly moving doors set flush in a stone arch-way. It is this type of architecture, the lack of our projecting steps, the flatness of doors and windows which give me at any rate the effect in certain quarters of Paris of living in a fortified city. Within the house was a broad winding stair-case built beautifully in an open well so that one might stand on the ground floor and glimpse the roof ceiling. It was the only beautiful thing in that house. Within two days I found it was not so "romantic" to live in a courtyard for the sun practically never penetrated the house. Oh that dampness! I, fresh from America with its steam heat and its auxiliary appliances of gas and oil, gas logs and accessible fireplaces, could understand Esau's quittance of his birthright for a mess of pottage. I'd have handed over the birth-rights of all my friends and relations for an ordinary gas heater with fixtures.

Incidentally I do not "get" the French attitude toward this matter of heating. Of course for a few extra daily cents I was able to get thawed out in the pension. They made a fire in my room of "*charbons*"—a sort of charcoal nugget of a beautiful oval shape. But they made it with surprise. "No one has a fire yet, Mademoiselle". The hotels advertise *chauffage centrale* (central heating) but of my dozen acquaintances who live in hotels only one bears testimony to the turning on of that heat. And that, she declares, produces an effect more by auto-suggestion than by actual warmth. A clever American who has lived in Paris for several years tells me that hotel-keepers say: "Oh yes we have central heating but of course the heat is not turned on yet because the winter hasn't really come". This sort of thing keeps up till the middle of January when the refrain changes to: "Well it isn't worth while turning it on now for it will soon be spring!" I think there is something to this story for when I came to this hotel my first inquiries were with regard to heat. The manager said "naturally the heat is not turned on yet". The garcon, Albert, expressed some surprise at my desire for a fire in my room and explained as he made it that the heat would be turned on tomorrow. A week later, the maid, in response to a searching inquiry, declared that the heat would be turned on soon. "Tomorrow?" I asked with an interest purely academic for my wood-fire was merrily blazing. "Oh, no not tomorrow", she rejoined aghast at the thought of setting so close a date, "but certainly within a few days".

In the pension a line from a melancholy hymn of my Presbyterian childhood comes back to me: "Change and decay in all around I see". The dining-room was negligible with a sort of shabby comfort. But the salon spoke of the decayed grandeur of other days. It was white and gold; a soiled white and a cracked and faded gold. There were many tapestried chairs reduced to a monotone of dinginess and innumerable knic-knacs and bibelots such as I have not seen since in that same childhood I visited the homes of various great-aunts. And about the boarders there was this same air of desiccation. An old, old lady, a widow I judged from her deep black and her son of perhaps 55; another old lady, once the matron I should say of some frightfully corrective institution, erect and with a terrible, raucous voice; four or five depressed young men, bookkeepers, clerks, hopelessly nondescript. The food was nondescript too.

Life in the pension is not French life only; it is life everywhere in similar environment. Only I had not thought of finding it in France.

Rue de Sèvres which leads from the Boulevard Montparnasse, where my friends live, to my street is an impressively busy place. There are all sorts of businesses here jumbled close side by side, delicatessens, bakeries, milliners' establishments, hardware stores, jewelers, photographers, a cutlery. Out of the apparent confusion rises gradually some appreciation of the unexpectedly hard common sense of the French which says: "One has to have all these things in order to live; why not have them all close at hand?" One would never have to walk a mile for a camel here either a literal or a figurative one. If French people elected to use camels they would be found, I am quite sure, along Rue de Sèvres tethered a bit too near perhaps to the exposed cheeses and the cuts of meat. It is this decidedly logical hard matter-of-factness which is, I am beginning to think, the Frenchiest quality about the French. One sees it cropping out in all sorts of ways. This is the sort of thing which is at once back of the spectacle of the irreproachably dressed householder emerging from the bakery with a large half loaf of bread tucked unwrapped under his arm and that other different spectacle of the exposure of the human form upon the French stage to a degree totally unparalleled by any theatre in America. "Life", says the Frenchman without cynicism, "is bread and is also shining flesh. Why bother to wrap up the one or to disguise the other?"

Such busy people! Gone in this section of the city at least is that illusion of Paris the play-ground of the world. I have never seen people work so hard in my life nor with such seriousness. It is true that they lose the time from twelve or twelve-thirty until two every day. Small shops close; the manicurist with a glance at her clock cannot do your hands now for see "it will take forty-five minutes at least. It is half-past eleven now and I close at twelve. Some other time perhaps mademoiselle?" But the remaining hours! Suzanne, the maid at the pension, eyes my trunk dubiously. "I am not sure that I can carry it up, Mademoiselle; I may have to call the concierge"! Albert in the hotel carries terrible trunks, loads and loads of heavy, heavy linen, huge baskets of wood,—all day, all day he trudges up and down, apparently never thinking of using the elevator. His aspect is not the least bit servile yet I do not remember seeing any one so consciously a servant. Or perhaps his heavy air is due to a dull inner wonderment. "Was it for this I crouched day and night in the trenches?" I have heard Dr. Du Bois speak many times of that something in colored Americans which simply will not let them work too long or too hard. That has been God's greatest gift.

Yet there is something about Paris. In the beginning I said that life in Paris is the same as life the civilized world over but that there was one exception. In Paris I find myself more American than I ever feel in America. I am more conscious of national characteristics than I have ever been in New York. When I say: "We do that differently in America," I do not mean that we do that differently in Harlem, or on "You" Street in Washington, or on Christian Street in Philadelphia. I mean that Americans white and black do not act that way. And I recall now as I write that practically all the public buildings here bear on them the legend: "Liberté, Egalité, Fraternité". I was busy at lunch-time today and so missed my dejeuner. *I shall go out presently and have tea and I shall have it at the first tea room which takes my fancy.* This is also something to be considered in reviewing French "life as she is".

THIS WAY TO THE FLEA MARKET

My friend said: "I think you ought to visit the Flea Market." I looked at her with amazement and some distaste for I was still smarting under the memory of my encounter with one of the pests during my first few days in Paris.

Presently she explained. Just outside of one of the gates of Paris—for Paris being a fortified city has several gates—there is held every Sunday from nine until four, a vast bazaar called the "*Marché aux Puces*", the "Flea Market", where one may buy all sorts of articles at considerable advantage. Originally the name was given because only very old and usually stolen wares were put on sale. But now both old and new objects are to be had and the market is a fully recognized and legitimate business.

Accordingly the next Sunday I started for the Porte de Clignancourt and the Marché aux Puces. My friend's father to accompany me, not only to show me the way but also to do the bargaining. "You look too easy", said my candid friend, "you need some one to look them in the eye and beat them at their own game for the moment they spy a foreigner they immediately raise the price."

The father, a sturdy, grizzled, kindly Alsatian, was not at all like the Alsatian shepherd boy of the song. Indeed had I seen him in America I should have taken him without further thought for German. Thus constantly are shaken my preconceptions with regard to the appearance of the French; they run so persistently contrary to type, that is to the type which we are told in America they most resemble. My guide knew his own neighborhood thoroughly and took me to a small Savings Bank, open for deposit on Sunday; to a church and, most interesting of all, to a small carpenter-shop designed for youngsters where boys of all sorts and conditions were happily engaged in drawing and planing and hammering. "Some of them", said their instructor, "do it for fun and others because they have a genuine feeling for the trade." This shop was part of a large school for poor children. Compulsory education has just been established in France and has been taken up with great thoroughness; in this one ward are fifty-two such institutions! Not only is the instruction free,—an innovation for the French,—but a luncheon is served gratis to the pupils every day.

At last we boarded the tramway and rode the length of Boulevard Ornano to the Porte de Clignancourt and the Flea Market. I was not impressed at first for I saw to one side only a few booths, very much as we see sometimes on the East Side in New York, and on these booths were exhibited very ordinary articles of commerce,—neckties, soap, powder, stockings. But presently the boulevard halted, vanished, to reappear in a broad muddy plain covered entirely with tents, booths, portable shops, vans, even desolate automobiles. There was visible a rough sort of plan; lanes ran between a double line of counters, to be met at right angles by other lanes; you could see that you really were in a market with the grey French sky for covering and the deep sticky mud beneath your feet. That mud! There is no mud I am convinced like unto French mud; it is black, it is viscous, it is thick, yet somehow it contrives to spatter and to penetrate and is "of a wetness"!

But the clientele of the Marché aux Puces did not care about mud. Nor did I,—there were far too many other things to consider. Not even in a big department store do I remember such a variety of objects. As far I can recall there were no fruits or vegetables, nor indeed any edibles except some cough candy made from the dried berries of the eucalyptus tree. I bought some of this as safeguard against the effects of the mud and as it tasted like a mixture of camphor and menthol I suppose it would hardly come in the category of edibles. But they were the only objects missing.

Very often as I gaze around the interior of a large shop catering as modern stores do to an appreciable portion of the increasing number of our needs, I wonder what Adam and Eve would think if they might spy just once the first aids to living which civilization has gathered about itself. They would, I think, murmur: "But we lived without any of these things! After all, Life is the important, the supreme end of existence; how can people be encompassed about with all these gee-gaws and yet find time to live?" Some such thought came to me at the Flea Market. Here were dolls, rain-coats, shoe-blacking, underwear, perfumes, oil-paintings, rugs, blankets, vases, china, shoes, bicycles, old suits of clothes, hats, fans, candle-sticks, discarded curtain fixtures, table-mats, telephone boxes, cutlery, old-time firing pieces, swords, poniards, daggers, canes, rabbit-skins,—my pen wearies of the enumeration.

Some of the wares were old, some perfectly new; some absolutely useless. Yet people were searching restlessly, feverishly through heaps of fixtures, rusty and even broken. Perhaps some hoped to find and to purchase for a few sous the one contrivance lacking to a world-astounding invention. The piles of worn and faded and altogether horrible clothing also had their devotees. Somehow I felt that it was from these garments and their too probable inhabitants that the market received its name. But the customers who would even envisage the thought of buying and wearing those garments could not afford to be too fastidious! The poor of Europe are very poor; they approach in the candor and simplicity of their idea of living the Adam and Eve of my conjecture. Life, the mere business of living, is their supreme occupation, let its trappings be as sordid, as infected, as repellant as may be; so long as the precious jewel of life is contained therein, what matter? It is a hard philosophy, but an inevitable one in a people who have fought so long and so often for the right to survive; and it is philosophy too, mind you, born of terrific experiences, not a mere dumb, driven acquiescence of the inequalities of life.

Buying and selling at the Flea Market is great game. Every body haggles. The merchant to whom a customer handed over the amount of his first price would despise him even while enjoying the thought of his gain. My

Alsatian friend had come from Mulhouse; hence when he picked up a picture showing the spires of the Cathedral of Strasburg and storks resting thereon, his rather impassive face quickened. He knew those surroundings; he had lived in Paris now for thirty-five years, but this,—this was home. He asked the price. "Twenty francs", replied the merchant in a hard, unyielding tone. He was a psychologist; he knew that one would want that picture only for its associations; but it is for this sort of thing that men pay dear.

My friend was unimpressed. "What is your final price?" he inquired succinctly.

"Eighteen francs."

"I'll give you ten."

The merchant did not even look up and we sauntered on very slowly for my friend knew that the end was not yet.

Presently came a loud "pst!" We returned.

"I'll let you have it for eighteen francs."

"I told you I'd give you ten." Complete suspension of interest on the part of the vendor. We started off again.

"Hey, here's your picture!" The ten francs and the painting crossed the counter. The picture was unwrapped and I wondered a little about this but my friend was prepared. He dived into a pocket and pulled out a newspaper in which he wrapped his purchase. Always bring a newspaper with you to the Marché aux Puces, he counseled; not enough profit is expected to admit of furnishing paper and string.

The women merchants are the hardest bargainers, seldom if ever yielding. I bought a rose and black beaded table mat at a price equivalent to one-third its cost in New York. My guide started to bargain with the woman who was selling, but her figure was her first and last. Some bantering followed: "You know I've got to live, Monsieur."

"Yes, but you shouldn't try to make all your profit on me."

"I'm not trying to." Shrewdly. "It isn't necessary for you to have the mat, but it is necessary for me to make my living. *Il faut vivre, Monsieur.*"

And not one sou would she yield. I was glad she would not. Her attitude, her calmness, her determination even to the point of grimness is characteristic of this class. There is something tremendously hard and stratified in the French character, a granite-like quality which results from this continuous necessity of being at grips with life itself. One always comes back to some evidence of that, the struggle for existence, the struggle with the soil and the struggle to keep the soil. And this struggle with its resulting hardness shows nowhere more plainly than in the poor and middleclass French woman. It is an extension of that instinct which makes the small and cornered animal fight so bitterly, converting him finally into a truly formidable opponent. Woman being the weaker creature must harden herself proportionately just that much more to meet the exigencies of her existence.

The vast quantity and profusion of merchandise scattered about intrigued of course my attention. But what really held me was the people; all sorts of a given class, with here and there a curious visitor like myself and my friend, but otherwise representatives of the poorer groups of all those nationalities with which Paris teems. Many of the merchants were Poles and Russians, but among the changing crowds of customers were Greeks, Italians, Spanish, Tunisians, Algerians, Annamites, Chinese, Kabyles. These last formed a striking and easily detected group. They were all thin, all swarthy with a swarthiness different from that of the Italian, the American mulatto, or the Spaniard. They wore dull red fezzes, their hair was lank and oily, their faces grimed; yet even so one received an impression of pride and aloofness. They made me think of sick eagles. Old clothes were their lodestone. After fingering garments heavy with grease and dirt, they left them only to return and handle them once more. They were cold, poor things. Hardy sons of the desert they might be, yet not the least of such nostalgia as they felt could be traced back to an unvoiced sense of contrast between the dampness of a French winter and the baking sun of Africa.

By noon the crowd had doubled; by two it would be quadrupled; it would be difficult to twist one's way out of the narrow, muddy lanes; by three the haggling would have reached its height, for merchandise must be disposed of in order to facilitate departure. At five o'clock that vast muddy expanse would be as barren of booths and of people as the sea.

I was surprised that so much vacant land should be lying unused at the very approach to a great city; one would have expected clusters of houses, small businesses, gardens, streets and trees. But here was nothing but a trackless waste, the nearest houses towering aloofly, several hundred metres away. My friend told me that thus was the land left bare all around the city so that the approach of an army would readily be descried! This turned my thoughts again to the fortifications curving away from us enclosing the great proud city, the darling of the French, the Mecca of Europe, the glory of the world! Vast grey stone bastions, as tall as a two-story house, surrounded by a moat which could of necessity be flooded with water. "But we don't do that any more", said my companion, "since we have such wonderful cannon."

The walls were as fascinating as the people. "A fortified city," I murmured, "we never have them in America." "But you would have them", he replied grimly, "if you had the Germans for neighbors." Always that fear of invasion keeping the military spirit in France alive and green.

And on that thought we left the market, left the seething, swarming crowds and the sordid, prosaic wares. A laughing youngster offering us a box of shoe-blacking, opened the box and pretended to lick it, closing his eyes in an ecstasy because it was so good. "So shoe-blacking your favorite dish now", bantered my Alsatian, "and how does it taste?" "It's all right, my old one", grinned back the boy, "you'd better buy some for mademoiselle!"

In front of us against a wintry-silver sunlight rose the mosque-like towers of *Sacré Coeur*. "Come in", they beckoned, "you are welcome!" Behind us curved and closed the fortifications; viewed from this side they emanated security, protection. "Pass in", they murmured, "You are safe!"

DARK ALGIERS THE WHITE: PART I

ILLUSTRATED BY LAURA WHEELER

Marseille, which from Paris seemed to beckon, proved on our arrival to be pointing the other way. For across the Mediterranean which stretched careless and blue at the foot of the Rue de Cannebiére loomed Africa.

Perhaps that dream-land would never lie so near us again. Algiers was twenty-eight hours away, beyond a sea that smiled and faintly rippled: a sea warmed and gilded by the sun which had forsaken Paris; curtained and lighted at night by stars and constellations which we had never seen; mellowed by a saffron moon climbing from below the surface of the world to the warm, rich velvet of the sky.

Time spent a day and four hours in rolling back the curtain which separated our known from the unknown. Suddenly the ship stood still in the midst of a large and beautiful artificial harbor enclosed in a circular break-water. Before us stretched the jetty and on it flashed a moving picture of brown and black faces, red fezzes, white turbans, white burnouses, red blanket robes. All the strangeness and difference of that life which, starting far, far in the interior of Africa, yet breaks off so abruptly at the southern edge of the Mediterranean, rose instantly to meet us. Porters agile as monkeys swarmed up narrow rope ladders over the side of the ship; one of them whipped a gay handkerchief from his throat, passed it through the handles of our valises, threw the staggering load over his shoulder and abruptly started off. Through a lane of staring chattering faces we passed, entered a waiting car. In a moment we had sped from *Mustapha Inférieur*, the lower level of the city, to *Alger*, the city proper. Ten minutes later we had registered in the Hotel Oasis. For a few days we would be residents of Algiers, dwellers in Africa.

Alger la blanche! Algiers the White! White Algiers the French rightly call it. I shall never forget that first impression. The city rises white in tiers up the side of a hill, of many hills. The town is built in three layers, Mustapha Inférieur on a level with and slightly above the jetty; Alger the middle city; Mustapha Supérieur on the hill crests. The roads are white, and white and chalky the dust on the palm-trees that line the streets and dot the public gardens. And on all sides swarm white clad patriarchal figures, superb in burnous and swathing turban. Staff in hand they make one think according to his training of pictures seen in Sunday School or film-shown "Scenes from an Eastern Village". Dark figures clad in European clothes but crowned with red fezzes bring East and West together. Down the Boulevard de la République shine the white minarets of an Arabian mosque. In the public square in front rises the statue of the Duc d'Orléans, the shoulders and the head showing flat like card-board against the sky.

It was nearly dusk when we left the hotel to catch the first glimpse of the city. We boarded an open trolley-car and rode to its terminus. It was a trolley-car of many turnings whose conductor, a courteous young Arab, took his task as a game. From the running-board he dashed to the pavement to turn on innumerable signal lights; he ran ahead and opened switches; from the gathering darkness friends hailed him and he made cheery responses. Some of them leaped on and rode a short distance. Either this traction company furnished endless passes or the young conductor considered this his treat, for his gay companions paid him nothing. Down on the sidewalk the white dust showed grey and grey walls showed dimly through grey air and suddenly appearing from around a turning and vanishing again in the misty night came mysterious figures of women clothed in white and numerous garments, a white face veil covering mouth and nose, cheeks and hair, all but two dark impenetrable eyes and a triangle of creamy forehead. An Arab in irreproachable "sack" suit and red fez mounted our trolley, first helping on his young wife. Mystery shrouded her; her two eyes stared unseeingly before her; she was like an automaton beside her lord; there was no conversation. When they dismounted we saw that her robe was wonderfully soft and white; that the stockings encasing her dainty ankles were faintly pink; that her shoes were russet and delicate. Before we ourselves descended an old woman came and sat opposite and we found a chance to examine her face veil. It seemed to be made of a piece of soft embroidered muslin shaped very much like the tiny white apron which a good American housewife sometimes assumes on a leisurely afternoon. The old Arabian woman's face was sallow and wrinkled. The triangle of flesh appearing above those faded eyes could scarcely ever have been smooth, so crissed and crossed was it now by a pattern of tiny lines. But old and faded and wrinkled as she was her clothing and her veil lent her mystery and marvel. She was the very savor of the East.

The morning brought its measure of disenchantment. Algiers was still white, still different, still mysterious but the merciless sun revealed its defects and destroyed its magic. The white burnouses were not quite so white, the flowing robes terminating a foot from the ground afforded a glimpse of European trousers and shoes; the children were sore-eyed; there were beggars at every corner. Through the voluminous garments of the women showed the outline of misshapen bodies, broken and distorted by neglect, abuse and much bearing of children. Yet nothing could destroy, could penetrate their air of mystery. And the grave and regal bearing of the better type of Arab compensated for the shocking anomaly of his dress. This anomaly showed everywhere, in the jostling of streets bearing now Arabic, now French names; in the issuing of

French sounds from bearded Arab lips; there were boulevards vaulted and arcaded like the Rue de Rivoli in Paris and just off them tier on tier of worn, crumbling steps which led to the dark and tortuous "native" quarters. So completely had my first glimpse of the city prepared me for a manifestation of life totally different from any which I had ever known that I was heart-broken at finding myself before an array of shops, in front of ranks of counters covered with jewels, bric-a-brac, pictures, gloves, materials such as one encounters any day in the Boulevard des Italiens or in Forty-second Street. It was unnecessary to close one's eyes to imagine oneself in Paris or New York.

Presently we find the courage to mount those worn and crumbling stairs which lead from spacious Rue Bab-Azoun and to emerge into the first street which lies back of it. Here immediately one is in another world.

The pavements are lined with shops and with booths, square and dark these last, some of them mere cubby-holes. In one, fezzes, gay handkerchiefs and meretricious jewelry is sold. The next is devoted to string. Algiers seems a center of the cord-making industry. Here a dark interior is lined with flaming bolts of cloth printed in crude, high colors; a little Arab, or perhaps he is a Turk, sits impassive behind a brief counter and dreams with wide staring velvet eyes beyond his shop, beyond the facing houses, perhaps beyond the sea. He does not see you as you pass by; from his expression I judge he will sell nothing today. Further down we enter a tiny dark shop; this one has windows displaying indifferently gay beads and faded basketry, a few bracelets showing in filagree Moorish emblems, the crescent and the hand of Fatmah. The spare grizzled proprietor shows us his wares. A passenger on the boat had warned us never to pay the first price mentioned. But we are Westerners. We do not haggle easily. He rejects with dignity our one timed suggestion at reduction. But the price is absurdly small in any case and we come away content

This street and all the streets in Algiers swarm with people—children, boys, and men, men, men! I have never seen so many not even in New York. They pass perpetually through the ways on the pavements and in the road; they sit in the native business quarters, on the edges of the side walk; they spill over into the gutters; they swarm the stone winding staircases which bisect the streets. Boys perched on stools eat couscous, the native dish, from a bowl or from a tin cup. Men magnificently bronzed, lean and regal, a red cloak streaming behind them, thunder by on—obviously—Arabian steeds. It is too bad that moviedom has spoiled the integrity of this scene; our sophisticated eyes find in it a touch of artificiality.

By accident the artist of our group and I stumble into a magnificent shop on Rue Bab-Azoun. We enter to purchase a trifling souvenir; we remain to finger, to envy and to listen to the expounding of "Pohoomull Brothers, Brahmin merchants". They are of course East Indians. I notice a curious phenomenon: the brothers are brown, we are brown, the Arabs are brown, but there is a difference in our brownness, so much so that clad all of us in Western dress, each would shortly be able to discriminate. The Pohoomull brothers greet us cordially; they call us "friends";

they order for us sweet, black Turkish coffee and Turkish cigarettes. They are delighted to show us a brooch in pearls and sapphires at 3000 francs, and minute and useless souvenirs at three. The more talkative partner leads us to a store-room of brasses and coppers; finely carved trays and vases; gorgeous incense burners; chimes, tables inlaid with copper and silver, cunning and unusual patterns wrought on knives and jugs and utensils whose uses we do not know. We assure him again and again that we have no intention of buying, that we are really quite poor. But he insists that it is a pleasure to him, that we are his "friends", that something in the shape of our heads makes him recognize kindred spirits and that therefore he would do for us what he would do for few others: show us in detail his 3,000,000 francs worth of merchandise and count it time well-spent. He makes me think of Forster's Dr. Aziz in his "Passage to India". The social amenities, he thinks, constitute friendship and when we in our tongue-tied Western fashion express our gratitude, for his belongings are marvellous and the atmosphere of his shop gracious and charming, he becomes more and more eager to please. He would do anything to make our stay in Algiers profitable and pleasant. Is there anything we desire; if it is not in his shop he will procure it elsewhere. He is so obviously sincere that my friend voices her great longing to paint a Moorish woman. The very thing—every day a number of girls come to his place to do embroidery—Pohoomull Brothers manufacture their own goods—"if Mademoiselle will look in tomorrow—". Mademoiselle does look in tomorrow—three times, but the girls are not there. "You can never depend on them", he apologizes, shaking his head in sorrow.

DARK ALGIERS THE WHITE: PART II

ILLUSTRATED BY LAURA WHEELER

DARK ALGIERS THE WHITE

JESSIE FAUSET

DRAWINGS BY LAURA WHEELER

In two parts: PART II

Those worn, winding stairs intrigue me. They savor of old-world necessities when men lent themselves painfully to the vagaries of nature instead of bending her to their comfort. It is possible mounting thus from one level to another to reach the very crests of the city. I start out along a twisting, writhing street, les Tournants de Rorigo, which winds circularly around itself always ascending the hill. At times I make a short cut to the next round by the simple expedient of climbing one of the steep stair-cases. I am obsessed with this serpentine street and must know what lies at the far end. There are not many Arabs here yet one meets them constantly always descending from above; there must be a colony of them up in the hill tops; perhaps the French drove them there when they took the city a century or so ago. I stop in a small bakery which oddly enough carries a side line in leather to buy a narrow red collar for a certain spoiled kitten in far-off New York and I ask the woman if it is safe for me to climb further. She assures me: “You may go anywhere, anywhere, Mademoiselle, and then besides one sees that you are from Martinique (Martiniquaise) and there is no danger here for a French woman!” Fortified I start again and almost at the top of the hill turn this time down a flight of steps and from a stone landing look into a miniature village some twenty feet below. There are perhaps a dozen houses here, or no, not houses, miserable shacks, swarming with women and children. They are unspeakably dirty and ragged yet somehow they strike a picturesque exotic note which makes me long for my artist friend. These women are without face veils; one of them passing directly before me wears a head-dress of searlet, a green jacket with a purple collar, a cerise and yellow skirt. Another is dressed from head to foot in various shades of red. A woman carrying a copper water jug on her shoulder crowns her brown garment with a splendid turban of yellow and gold. I cannot sufficiently describe the picture they made in their gay clothing, the brilliant blue of the sky above, the strong gold of the sun above them, the black background of squalor and wretchedness behind. The farthest possibilities of mankind meet in them. A French woman mounting from below stops by my side a moment and tells me that this is “The Court of Miracles”. But she is unable to explain the reason for this palpable irony.

She points to still another flight just a few feet away. “That leads to the Kasbah, the Arab quarter. If you really want to see the natives, how they live—they are there.” Of course I want to see them, so I descend and mount again. This time I am in a world as different from lower Algiers as that world in turn is from New York. I am suddenly in a network of narrow, narrow, winding lanes—they are too small for streets for their entire width is not that of a New York side-walk. The lanes are paved, they keep a tortuous pattern which my inexperienced eye can glimpse but cannot follow. The houses on either side touch in their second and third stories so that one is constantly passing under square or vaulted arches. A few doors are open and loitering I spy in a dark interior a form bending intently over a wheel, a tiny lamp illuminating just the inch of work on which the artisan is painfully engaged. Once I catch a glow which lights up a whole room—there is a bake-oven here; in another door-way boys are twisting cord—one of them makes a spindle of his toe.

Dark and narrow as these lanes are there are those still darker and narrower, not wide enough for two people to pass without brushing shoulders. I do not enter any of these, indeed I am beginning to be conscious of a slowly mounting fear; I follow the pattern of streets, downward, downward in the direction of the sea where I know there is light and safety. I restrain an impulse to run and walk very erectly, very swiftly past the pinkish stone houses with their heavy small arched doors, closed so tightly; past groups of Arabs gambling; a French soldier overtaking me looks at me curiously; three well dressed Arabs, their burnouses snowy, their turbans gaily bound, pass me, then stop and look back. But clearly I have a definite goal, for I branch off suddenly and proceed still downward in another direction. And suddenly I am out at three o'clock of a brilliant January afternoon in a fairly broad street, still full of strange faces, but open to the sky and affording glimpses of the blessed sea.

I come back the next day with my friends, the artist and the student. We peer fearfully into the Cour des Miracles then halt at the foot of the stairs leading up to the Kasbah so that the artist may make a note of Arab children at play. As we stand a French woman, leading her little girl who has been intently regarding us for some moments, comes closer and asks me if we are thinking of visiting the quarters. And when I say yes she exclaims: "Not without an escort!" I tell her proudly that I had gone through the day before by myself. "Bon Dieu", she cries and tells me of terrible possible happenings, the tragedies of those sinister, black off-shoots and allies. She leads us out by a path that skirts the quarters and while the artist stops again promises that if I will come back the next afternoon she and her husband who is on the police force will show me about. If her husband should be on duty she will take me into one or two of the shops on the outskirts.

A rambling, crazy little trolley deposits me the next day at the very top of the hill. The French barracks is on one side and three or four Sentinels are on patrol. My heart fails me at first for my guide does not appear and the sight of the strange bronzed faces regarding me curiously as I stand a lonely equally exotic figure in the middle of the sunlit road unnerves me.

I have lost the courage which saw me through my first visit, the Frenchwoman's warnings have undermined it. Presently she and her little girl arrive, her husband is on duty, but there are one or two places where the two of us may pass in safety, and the French soldiers are all around. We enter first the Moorish cemetery of El Kettar which is built on an abruptly dropping terrace so thickly studded with tombs that one has scarcely a footing. Rich and poor are crowded together, the tombstones are mostly flat, with here and there an iron grill. Nothing more unlike our carefully kept cemeteries can be imagined. We turn then and walking past the barracks and along a hill crest winding circularly above the sea come slowly back to the same staircase of the Kasbah where I had first so bravely entered.

To my astonishment my little French friend stops before one of those heavy rounded doors, pushes it easily open, beckons for me to follow and I am actually in an Arab house in the Kasbah. This is the home she tells me of a Moorish friend of hers, Fatmah. And calling the name loudly she leads me through a short, dark hall into a small courtyard and up a narrow winding stairway done in worn but beautiful tiles in old blue, red and yellow. At the first turn of the staircase we come to a curtained door opening on a dark oblong room five feet perhaps by eight. In a moment my eyes, accustomed to the gloom, pick out three figures of women sitting on the floor near a brazier of live coals. Their backs are against the wall, their feet are bare, their hands are in their laps. They sit thus, listless, doing nothing, absolutely nothing; life slips by. Fatmah is not there; a tiny woman, the oldest of the group, greets my French friend and conducts us to a house in another lane a dozen feet away. Arab families live, I am told, as far as possible under one roof. If this is not feasible they seek adjoining houses. In this case Madame Fatmah, her sister Madame Kheira and their brother occupy three of the tiny dwellings. Madame Kheira's house which we now visit is fairly tall. Back of the inevitable heavy door is the equally inevitable court yard lighted from a skylight flush with the roof of the house. The winding cement stairway gives on a narrow balcony in the back of which is a door leading again into a dark oblong room. Here we sit and wait for the still elusive Fatmah. The old lady, Fatmah's mother, is courteous and incurious; a young girl, Fatmah's niece, is frankly curious but still courteous. I sit Arab fashion on pillows on the floor and look about me. The place is very clean, the walls are done in flat high blue, a bed of old brass covered with magenta showing through coarse lace fills one end of the room, a sort of high-boy bearing a dish of oranges takes up the other. A wooden scimitar carved in dull red and blue hangs high on one wall and near it a small picture of a brilliant peacock. Two cats and a dog join our group as we exchange polite and amiable banalities after the fashion of ladies calling the world over.

Fatmah's niece directs us to the "terrace" which is really the roof of the room on the second floor. We have to mount a stair-case without balustrade like a steeply set ladder but the climb is worth while for the terrace affords a new view of the Mediterranean and a far-off shadowy cape. The two cats have followed us and are met by two others above. The four of them, one yellow, one black and white, one grey and one a handsome white imperfectly valeted, are absolutely unobtrusive but they do like human company. Fatmah comes at last closely trailed by her brother's little boy. She is wrinkled yet not old, busy, purposeful, industrious, a perfect Martha to the Mary of her sister Madame Kheira who comes to complete our group. Kheira is beautiful, her wonderful purple eyes are set slanting, their lashes are long and curling, her skin is the color of cream. The slightly accentuated lines of the mouth give her face character without age, otherwise she is unwrinkled. Her hair dyed a dark henna is perfection with her mat skin. I stare at her in such complete absorption that her glorious eyes finally question me and I blurt out: "You are so beautiful, Madame; I wish my artist friend could see you."

She smiles but receives the compliment without self-consciousness with the serene assurance indeed of an acknowledged belle. Her clothes are terrible, mere shapeless bloomers and a blouse or two, but they lose their grotesqueness surmounted by that perfectly chiselled face.

There was a little table about a foot and a half high on the terrace which I took to be a child's toy, but we pass within to another dark oblong room and there is the little table bearing a coffee service—a copper pot on a brass and copper tray chiselled and engraven like the ones in the shop of "Pohoomull Brothers". The Moorish women leave their shoes at the threshold and we sit on the floor about the doll table and drink thick sweet coffee from small handle-less cups. It is time for me to go. I rise and thank them: "Vous êtes trés aimables, Mesdames; je vous remercie beaucoup." "Oh no," they reply, "it is we who thank you." Our politeness is that of Paris. "Au revoir Mademoiselle and good luck." They crowd the dark doorway and watch me. "She is really very nice (gentille)", says Kheira. I turn and wave—a curve blots them out. I am on the safe highway again waiting for the Toonerville trolley.

My French friend waits with me. I do not know how to thank her for she has given me a rare afternoon such as I could never have procured at the hands of a guide. I ask if I may give her little girl a present. But blushing deeply she refuses. "It was a pleasure; you were so interested." I thank her again; my trolley appears. Our eyes dwell on each other with the glance of people whose lives for an hour have touched deeply at their only possible tangent. In spite of our good wishes and our expressions of au revoir we never expect to meet again.

In the morning, midway in hurried packing I hear a tap on my door. I cry "Entrez", and there she stands with her inevitable little girl. I am so amazed that I can hardly greet her. Downcast, dejected she offers me a bit of grimy paper bearing a few names. "A friend of mine," she stammers, "her husband broke his leg; we are getting up a subscription for her and I thought of you." She is so embarrassed! We fancy that her husband has sent her—"She was an American and you showed her about all afternoon and never got a penny from her. Catch her before she sails!" We are sorry for her plight, it is so clearly not of her own choosing. I give her the francs which she so richly deserves and return a hearty welcome to her profuse and apologetic thankfulness. The child says greedily, "Give them to me maman." Once more we exchange adieu. But our little idyl has a tarnished ending.

Algiers the White! gateway to the deeper mysteries of Africa and of the East. Beyond lies the desert and the villages of the Kabyles. A few hours' ride from this seaport and we should be in the midst of strange exotic cities with new fantastic names, Blida, Bongie, Bou-Sâada and Biskra. Timgad, Laghouat and Touggourt; the gorges of Chiffa and the Ruisseau des Singes, the river of Monkiesii.

"ONCE MORE WE EXCHANGE ADIEU"

We tell our headwaiter, an elegant, serious young Frenchman with dead white skin and intense black hair, that we have never tasted the native dish, couscous. So he serves it as a specialty one night for dinner. It is not as new and different as bouillabaisse, the fish soup which we get in Marseille; it is really only a glorified stew of mutton, semoule (a cereal like farina), beans and peas. As this gorgeous climate affords three crops a year the vegetables are delicious.

On our last Sunday the artist and I strolling through the Faubourg Bab El Oued into the public square of the Place du Gouvernement pause to watch the Arabs filing by twos and threes for prayer into the Grand Mosque, Djama El Kebir. With one accord we pass in too, and removing our shoes, kneel in the dim silence on the great prayer carpet and with faces turned toward the rising of the sun breathe a prayer to the God who watches alike over East and West.

One picture is typically the East. I turn suddenly from the noise of Rue Marengo to the spacious and wide staircase leading into the Rue Sidi-Abderrah-Mane et-Tsalbi. A bronze, lean beggar, a very patriarch of beggars, sits at the top of these steps in the warm January sun-light. Above him rises a stone railing and above the railing show palms and orange trees. His hand stretched out he remains perfectly immobile: he does not look at the passersby, he does not solicit any alms. I watch him for five minutes and nothing about him moves but his eye-lids. A woman, white robed, half-veiled zig-zags up the steep stairs; her feet are thrust in high-heeled red slippers, she is stockingless but her ankles are concealed by silver bracelets four inches wide set with bright opaque red stones.

Again the porter slips his neckerchief through the handles of our bags and precedes us up the gang way of the steamer Timgad. The machinery starts up, the shore-hands cast off. A young Moorish monk beside us, his unshaven beard showing coal black against the soft tan of his face, waves a sad repressed farewell to someone on the jetty. We get up steam; Mustapha Inférieur vanishes; the bay is lost; Cape Matifou, farthest outlying point of the coast, fades into spray and mist. Algiers, Africa, again are dreams.

Faithfully Yours, Jessie Redmon Fauset

Villefranche-sur-Mer
27 January, 1925

THE EUCALYPTUS TREE

A Reverie of Rome, the Catacombs, Christianity and the Moving Beauty of Italy

Rome. Iron and blood. And tears. I had expected the iron; those Gallic wars which once I had read and taught had so prepared me. And I should not have been too astounded if I had seen the little Tiber running red. But I had not looked for tears.

Along the far-famed Appian Way lie the Catacombs of Rome. Graves in which people, paradoxically, once lived! Terrible places! Tombs and worse than tombs! Little shelves, six feet long and pathetically narrow, cut in the dank dark earth; twenty-four feet of cubic soil to contain that which some day would once more be soil. Which now is soil.

One of those catacombs I shall never forget. St. Calixtus. We rode in the soft Italian January weather along that same Appian Way; three of us with a guide who spoke "fluent English". He pointed to figures in wayside shrines and called them "stachéls". Discoursing of legends built about Peter and Paul he differentiated between the two saints by using the formula of "this feller" and "that feller". We had hard work to keep serious countenances; his pompous assurance of his superb linguistic ability was overwhelming. Yet who were we to cavil, we whose knowledge of the language of Rome was confined to the formula: "Via est longa".

Without warning we stopped at a wide gate which led into a meadow, thickly studded with trees and brown moving figures. Monks. Men of God wearing sturdy thick brown robes, stiff and unyielding stuff. A mortification to both the flesh and the eye. Winding through these we came to a small room, not much more than a shed where the inevitable souvenirs were vended. A medley of things all impractical such as one sees at small seashore resorts. Strings and rosaries of translucent beads in luscious soft colorings; greens, lavenders and blues; numberless postcards, trinkets of all descriptions. Nearly all useless. And thick, stale, bitterly strong milk chocolate which the monks made and which for that reason, it seemed, should have been very good. In reality it nauseous. True tourists, we stopped and bought a few beads; a cake of the disappointing milk-chocolate. Then our guide came forward with a monk whose business it was to conduct parties through the catacombs. To each of us he handed a long slender yellowish wax taper and through a yawning doorway we entered literally into a hole in the ground. One moment we had been out in the open; the graciousness of air, the blueness of sky, endlessness of space about us. The next second we knew darkness, dankness, confinement. Just inside the doorway someone lit our tapers and then single file, awe-stricken, cold, we plunged down a few steep narrow steps into the bowels of the earth.

Death was about me. I knew it, I felt it. Old death echoing back from centuries before. Not the mere cessation of living but the death of high hopes, of burning love. The death that had been presaged by utter despair. On and on we paced through earthy passages; earthy, oozing ceilings above us; smooth, cold, earthy walls hemming us in. And in those walls those ghastly spaces where Christians had slept first the sleep of life and then the sleep of death. The guide's voice floated back down the narrow hall; his words couched in incomprehensible English were relayed to us by our guide of the "fluent tongue". We learned anew of the stories of men and women who had died simply and willingly for the cause of Christ. Who worse still had lived through nameless tortures of fire and water and shame for that same cause; stealing out to gatherings beneath the Italian moon; assembling fearfully in cypress groves and with great good luck returning through the midnight watches to their living tombs.

Our tapers flickered in the still, sullen air. If they should go out! But they continued to burn fitfully in some strange unison with the unevenly articulated tones of the monk. I cannot tell you what negation of existence as I knew it descended upon me as I stood there within earthen chamber, with only the faint glow of the taper between me and utter darkness and the knowledge and goodwill of the monk and the guide our one link between the sweet life going on above us, above ground where there were sweet air and sunlight and realities! To be lost in those subterranean passages, to wander ceaselessly groping through the dark, to have one's fingers encounter a dank case where a skeleton reposed! The slow dissolution of courage! The imminence of madness! Despair! Sudden death would be sweeter.

Turning a corner we came to a shallow three-walled chamber, on whose earthen floor reposed a lovely stone carving of beautiful beheaded St. Cecilia, the gift of parents of our time in memory of a daughter whom death had claimed too early. ... But its beautiful perfection is not for me; I will muse on it later; I will buy pictures of it, but now all my desire is to leave behind this horrible place and to find ... life.

And suddenly I am once more at the narrow steep stair-case, an inch of flaming taper still in my hand. The sweet world beckons. And just as I emerge from the door-way I spy the eucalyptus tree. It is green and perfect, towering a huge, graceful pyramid more than a hundred feet in air. A little wind coming across the meadow played through its flowing pendent leaves. From within its foliage I caught a faint continuous murmur, like the running of water. Like the running of a rivulet composed of all those tears which Christians had shed in those terrible days of doom and death. But the murmur of the wind rose above this like an obligato, like a chant of life, of endurance, of the immanence in Christianity of well-being and ultimate good. The tree, the eucalyptus tree, had caught and preserved the essence of all that the early martyrs had lavished so profusely on the iron pride of Rome. On the blood-stained prestige of Rome. Their goodness, their amazing faith, their tears. These things had been stronger than all the will of emperors and panoplied armies. The Christian Church now centres at Rome. The roots of the eucalyptus tree are plunged deep in that cemetery but its branches bear a beneficent sap within their veins. Baffled, beaten, its beginnings in catacombs of doubt, misinterpretation, tears, Christianity yet rises, rises with healing in its wings.

SOME NOTES ON COLOR

A distinguished novelist said to me not long ago: "I think you colored people make a great mistake in dragging the race problem into your books and novels. It isn't art."

"But good heavens," I told him, "it's life, it's colored life. Being colored is being a problem."

That attitude and the sort of attitude instanced by a journalist the other day who thought colored people ought to be willing to permit the term "nigger" because it carries with it so much picturesqueness defines pretty well, I think, our position in the eyes of the white world. Either we are inartistic or we are picturesque and always the inference is implied that we live objectively with one eye on the attitude of the white world as though it were the audience and we the players whose hope and design is to please.

Of course we do think about the white world, we have to. But not at all in the sense in which that white world thinks it. For the curious thing about white people is that they expect us to judge them by their statute-books and not by their actions. But we colored people have learned better, so much so that when we prepare for a journey, when we enter on a new undertaking, when we decide on where to go to school, if we want to shop, to move, to go to the theatre, to eat (outside of our own houses) we think quite consciously, "If we can pull it through without some white person interfering."

I have hesitated more than once about writing this article because my life has been spent in the localities which are considered favorable to colored people and in the class which least meets the grossest forms of prejudice. And yet—I do not say I would if I could—but I must say I cannot if I will forget the fact of color in almost everything I do or say in the sense in which I forget the shape of my face or the size of my hands and feet.

Being colored in America at any rate means: Facing the ordinary difficulties of life, getting education, work, in fine getting a living plus fighting everyday against some inhibition of natural liberties.

Let me see if I can give you some ideas. I am a colored woman, neither white nor black, neither pretty nor ugly, neither specially graced nor at all deformed. I am fairly well educated, of fair manners and deportment. In brief, the average American done over in brown. In the morning I go to work by means of the subway, which is crowded. Presently somebody gets up. The man standing in front of the vacant place looks around meaning to point it out to a women. I am the nearest one, "But oh," says his glance, "you're colored. I'm not expected to give it to you." And down he plumps. According to my reflexes that morning, I think to myself "hypocrite" or "pig." And make a conscious effort to shake the unpleasantness of it off, for I don't want my day spoiled.

At noon I go for lunch. But I always go to the same place because I an not sure of my reception in other places. If I go to another place I must fight it through. But usually I am hungry. I want food, not a lawsuit. And, too, how long am I to wait before I am sure of the slight? Shall I march up to the proprietor and say "Do you serve colored people?" or shall I sit and drum on the table for 15 or 20 minutes, feel my anger rising, prepare to explode only to have the attendant come at that moment and nonchalantly arrange the table? I eat but I go out still not knowing whether the delay was intentional or not. The white patron would be annoyed at the delay. I am, too, but ought I to be annoyed at something in addition to that? I can't tell. The uncertainty beclouds my afternoon.

An acquaintance—a white woman—phones me that she can accept a long-standing invitation of mine for luncheon. We meet and I suggest my old standby. "Let's go somewhere else," she urges. "I don't like that place."

Ruefully but frankly I stammer, "Well you see—I'm not quite sure—that is—"

"Oh, yes," she rejoins in quick pity. "I forgot that. I'm so sorry."

But I hate to be pitied even so sincerely. I hate to have this position thrust upon me.

All of us are passionately interested in the education of our children, our younger brothers and sisters. And just as deliberately, as earnestly as white people discuss tuition, relative ability of professors, expenses, etc., so we in addition discuss the question of prejudice. "Of course he'll meet someone. But would they let it interfere with his deserts? I don't know. I guess I'd better send him to A. instead of B. They don't cater as much to the South as at B."

I think the thing that irks us most is the teasing uncertainty of it all. Did the man at the box-office give us the seat behind the post on purpose? Is the shop-girl impudent or merely nervous? Had the position really been filled before we applied for it? What actuates the teacher who tells Alice — oh, so kindly—that the college preparatory course is really very difficult. Even remarkably clever pupils have been known to fail. Now if she were Alice—

Other things cut deeper, undermine the very roots of our belief in mankind. In school we sing "America," we learn the Declaration of Independence, we read and even memorize some of the passages in the Constitution. Chivalry, kindness, consideration are the ideals held up before us—

> "Honor and faith and good intent,
> But it wasn't at all what the lady meant."

the lady in this case being the white world. The good things of life, the true, the beautiful, the just, these are not meant for us.

So much is this difference impressed on us, "this for you but that quite other thing for me," that finally we come to take all expressions of a white man's justice with cynical disbelief, our standard of measure being a provident "How does he stand on the color question?"

I am constantly amazed as I grow older at the network of misunderstanding—to speak mildly—at the misrepresentation of things as they really are which is so persistently cast around us. Sometimes it is by implication, sometimes by open statement. Thus we grow up thinking that they are no colored heroes. The foreign student does hear of Garibaldi, of Cromwell, of Napoleon, of Marco Bozzaris. But neither he nor we hear of Crispus Attucks. There are no pictures of colored fairies in the story-books or even of colored boys and girls. "Sweetness and light" are of the white world.

Native Americans are "savages" owing their little knowledge of civilization to the kindly European traveler who is represented as half philanthropist, half savant. How much do we learn of indigenous African art, culture, morals? We are told of the horrors of polygamy without a word of the accompanying fact that prostitution in Africa was comparatively unknown—until the whites introduced it.

We are given the impression that we are the last in the scale of all races, that even other dark peoples will have none of us. I shall never forget how astonished I was to see in London at the second Pan-African Congress the very real willingness of Hindu leaders to cast in their lot with ours.

More serious still, we are constantly being confronted with a choice between expediency and intellectual dishonesty, intangible, indefinable and yet sometimes I think the greatest danger of all. If persisted in it is bound to touch the very core of our racial naturalness. And that is the tendency of the white world to judge us always at our worst and our own realization of that fact. The result is a stilled art and a lack of frank expression on our part. We find The Emperor Jones wonderful, but why couldn't O'Neill have portrayed a colored gentleman? We wish he had. "Batouala" is a marvellous piece of artistry, but we are half glad it is written in French so that the average white American won't insist that here is the true African prototype.

Some one will say: "These are trifles." What have I to complain of as compared with the condition of Negroes in South Africa, in Georgia, in the Portuguese possessions? I do not have to fear lynching, or burning, or dispossession.

No, only the reflex of those things. Perhaps it is mere nervousness, perhaps it is something more justifiable. Often when I am sitting in a crowded assembly I think, "I wish I had taken a seat near the door. If there should be an accident, a fire, none of these men around here would help me." Place aux dames was not meant for colored women.

I have not been dispossessed, but I have had to leave Philadelphia—the city of my birth and preference, because I was educated to do high school work and it was impossible for a colored woman to get that kind of work in that town. So I, too, have assisted in the Negro Exodus which the student of Sociology considers in class-room and seminary.

And so the puzzling, tangling, nerve-wracking consciousness of color envelops and swathes us. Some of us, it smothers.

POEMS

NOSTALGIA

Lonely log cabin
On the road to Nostalgia,
Sighing and sagging and quaking;
Let me breathe to the heart of your walls
A secret—
To keep it from breaking.
Once in a Harlem cellar,
A brown girl,
Wiggling and strutting
In a stranger's arms,
Dreaming of you
For a God-given moment—
Forget to proffer her charms.

EPISODE

The memory of you is slight in my mind,
But poignant.
Like a sole, unrepeated experience,
Like the wheeling flight of a gull,
Like smoke hanging high in the blue
In vaporish traceries,—
Without sound, but significant
As a thunder-preceding lull.

Once I remember glimpsing
A column of sand-pipers
Marching meticulously
Over the sedge-strewn floor of the beach;
Slight and graceful, unswerving
As war-going fifers;
Persistent, purposeful, sure,—
And just beyond reach!

Easily, far too easily
That picture fades from my senses;
Yet if once I recall it

There springs to my mind perfection;
Perfection of sky and sun
And ocean and weather
Promised fulfilment, of yearning,
Assurance of heaven's protection.
So you. The memory of you
Is slight but poignant;
Yet once you enter my mind
For the moment you sever
All my connection with paltriness,
Actions ignoble;
Leaving me peace and completeness.—
Remain with me ever!

DIVINE AFFLATUS

Tell me, swart children of the Southland
Chopping at cotton
In the sandy soil,
What do ye dream?
What deeds, what words of heroes
Leaven and lighten up
Your toil?
Know ye of L'Ouverture who freed a nation?
Heard ye of Crispus Attucks,
Or of Young?
Does fiery Vesey
Stir the spark within ye,
Or Douglass
Of the rare and matchless tongue?
That Washington
Who moulded a Tuskegee—
Does he inspire ye?
Does brave Moton thrill?
Mark ye Du Bois
That proud, unyielding eagle,
Beckoning ye higher than the highest hill?

But the swart children
Of the Southland
Stopping to dash the sweatbeads
From dull brows,
Answer: "These names
Mean nothing to us,
They, nor the unheard causes they espouse.
Only we know meek Jesus,
Thorn-encircled,
Broken and bleeding
In his Passion's toils;
And Lazarus
Sharing crumbs with dogs;
And Job,
Potsherd in hand, a-scraping at his boils!"

CHRISTMAS EVE IN FRANCE

Oh, little Christ, why do you sigh
As you look down tonight
On breathless France, on bleeding France,
And all her dreadful plight?
What bows your childish head so low?
What turns your cheek so white?

Oh, little Christ, why do you moan,
What is it that you see
In mourning France, in martyred France,
And her great agony?
Does she recall your own dark day,
Your own Gethsemane?

Oh, little Christ, why do you weep,
Why flow your tears so sore
For pleading France, for praying France,
A suppliant at God's door?
"God sweetened not my cup," you say,
"Shall He for France do more?"

Oh, little Christ, what can this mean,
   Why must this. horror be
For fainting France, for faithful France,
   And her sweet chivalry?
"I bled to free all men," you say,
   "France bleeds to keep men free."

Oh, little, lovely Christ-you smile!
   What guerdon is in store
For gallant France, for glorious France,
   And all her valiant corps?
"Behold I live, and France, like me,
   Shall live for evermore."

FRAGMENT

The breath of life imbued those few dim days!
Yet all we had was this,—
A flashing smile, a touch of hands, and once
A fleeting kiss.

Blank futile death inheres these years between!
Still naught have you and I
But frozen tears, and stifled words, and once
A sharp caught cry.

TOUCHÉ

Dear, when we sit in that high, placid room,
"Loving" and "doving" as all lovers do,
Laughing and leaning so close in the gloom,—

What is the change that creeps sharp over you?
Just as you raise your fine hand to my hair,
Bringing that glance of mixed wonder and rue?

"Black hair," you murmur, "so lustrous and rare,
Beautiful too, like a raven's smooth wing;
Surely no gold locks were ever more fair."

Why do you say every night that same thing?
Turning your mind to some old constant theme,
Half meditating and half murmuring?

Tell me, that girl of your young manhood's dream,
Her you loved first in that dim long ago
Had she blue eyes? Did her hair goldly gleam?

Does *she* come back to you softly and slow,

Stepping wraith-wise from the depths of the past?
Quickened and fired by the warmth of our glow?

There I've divined it! My wit holds you fast.
Nay, no excuses; 'tis little I care.
I knew a lad in my own girlhood's past,—
Blue eyes he had and such waving gold hair!

SONG FOR A LOST COMRADE

(To O.B.J.)

Oh the fields glint gold and the trees flare red,
    And the sky is as blue as the sky may be;
And the Past is past and the Dead are dead,
    And Life laughs in front of us fair and free!
        So it's, Ho Friends, a toast!
        Let us drink high together,
Pledging, Life, Love and Laughter, in the gay, gold weather!

True, alas, there is One that is gone from our throng,
    A Comrade to all and a good Friend was she;
And clear came her laughter and sweet rang her song—
    But now she lies hushed by the bent birch tree.
        She'd be first, Friends to cry:
        "Let us drink high together,
"Pledging, Life, Love and Laughter, in the gay, gold weather!"

Ah she raised Life's cup and drank of it, too,
    And Pain, like Joy, found a smile in her eye;

At all times most tender; to all trusts most true,
She had learned how to live, so she knew how to die.
Nay, no tears, Friends. A Toast:
Let us drink deep together,
Pledging, Life-long Remembrance, in the gay, gold weather!

RAIN FUGUE

Slanting, driving, Summer rain
How you wash my heart of pain!
How you make me think of trees,
Ships and gulls and flashing seas!
In your furious, tearing wind,
Swells a chant that heals my mind;
And your passion high and proud,
Makes me shout and laugh aloud!

Autumn rains that start at dawn,
"Dropping veils of thinnest lawn",
Soaking sod between dank grasses,
Sweeping golden leaves in masses,—
Blotting, blurring out the Past,
In a dream you hold me fast;
Calling, coaxing to forget
Things that are, for things not yet.

Winter tempest, winter rain,
Hurtling down with might and main,
You but make me hug my hearth,

Laughing, sheltered from your wrath.
Now I woo my dancing fire,
Piling, piling drift-wood higher.
Books and friends and pictures old,
Hearten while you pound and scold!

Pattering wistful showers of Spring
Set me to remembering
Far-off times and lovers too,
Gentle joys and heart-break rue,—
Memories I'd as lief forget,
Were not oblivion sadder yet.
Ah! You twist my mind with pain,
Wistful, whispering April rain!

Summer, Autumn, Winter rain,
How you ease my heart of pain!
Whispering, wistful showers of Spring,
How I love the hurt you bring!

LA VIE C'EST LA VIE

On summer afternoons I sit
Quiescent by you in the park,
And idly watch the sunbeams gild
And tint the ash-trees' bark.

Or else I watch the squirrels frisk
And chaffer in the grassy lane;
And all the while I mark your voice
Breaking with love and pain.

I know a woman who would give
Her chance of heaven to take my place;
To see the love-light in your eyes,
The love-glow on your face!

And there's a man whose lightest word
Can set my chilly blood afire;
Fulfillment of his least behest
Defines my life's desire.

But he will none of me, nor I
Of you. Nor you of her. 'Tis said
The world is full of jests like these—
I wish that I were dead.

DEAD FIRES

If this is peace, this dead and leaden thing,
   Then better far the hateful fret, the sting.
Better the wound forever seeking balm
   Than this gray calm!

Is this pain's surcease? Better far the ache,
   The long-drawn dreary day, the night's white wake,
Better the choking sigh, the sobbing breath
   Than passion's death!

ORIFLAMME

"I can remember when I was a little, young girl, how my old mammy would sit out of doors in the evenings and look up at the stars and groan, and I would say, 'Mammy, what makes you groan so?' And she would say, 'I am groaning to think of my poor children; they do not know where I be and I don't know where they be. I look up at the stars and they look up at the stars!'" —Sojourner Truth

I think I see her sitting bowed and black,
    Stricken and seared with slavery's mortal scars,
Reft of her children, lonely, anguished, yet
    Still looking at the stars.

Symbolic mother, we thy myriad sons,
    Pounding our stubborn hearts on Freedom's bars,
Clutching our birthright, fight with faces set,
    Still visioning the stars!

NOBLESSE OBLIGE

Lolotte, who attires my hair,
Lost her lover. Lolotte weeps;
Trails her hand before her eyes;
Hangs her head and mopes and sighs,
Mutters of the pangs of hell.
Fills the circumambient air
With her plaints and her despair.
Looks at me:
"May you never know, Mam'selle,
Love's harsh cruelty."

Love's dart lurks in my heart too,—
None may know the smart
Throbbing underneath my smile.
Burning, pricking all the while
That I dance and sing and spar,
Juggling words and making quips
To hide the trembling of my lips.
I must laugh
What time I moan to moon and star
To help me stand the gaff.

What a silly thing is pride!
Lolotte bares her heart.
Heedless that each runner reads
All her thoughts and all her needs.
What I hide with my soul's life
Lolotte tells with tear and cry.
Blurs her pain with sob and sigh.
Happy Lolotte, she!
I must jest while sorrow's knife
Stabs in ecstasy.

"If I live, I shall outlive."
Meanwhile I am barred
From expression of my pain.
Let my heart be torn in twain,
Only I may know the truth.
Happy Lolotte, blessed she
Who may tell her agony!
On me a seal is set.
Love is lost, and—bitter ruth—
Pride is with me yet!

THE RETURN

I that found the way so smooth
  With gilly-flowers that beck and nod,
Now find that same road wild and steep
  With need for compass and for rod,
And yet with feet that bleed, I pant
  On blindly—stumbling back to God!

WORDS! WORDS!

How did it happen that we quarreled?
We two who loved each other so!
Only the moment before we were one,
Using the language that lovers know.
And then of a sudden, a word, a phrase
That struck at the heart like a poignard's blow.
And you went beserk, and I saw red,
And love lay between us, bleeding and dead!
Dead! When we loved each other so!

How *could* it happen that we quarreled!
Think of the things we used to say!
"What does it matter, dear, what you do?
Love such as ours has to last for aye!"
—"Try me! I love to ensure your test!"
—"Love, we shall always love, come what may!"
What are the words the apostle saith?
"In the power of the tongue are Life and Death!"
Think of the things we used to say!

RENCONTRE

My heart that beat so passionless,
   Leaped high last night when I saw you.
Within me surged the grief of years
   And whelmed me with its endless rue.
My heart that slept so still, so spent,
   Awoke last night—to break anew.

RONDEAU

When April's here and meadows wide
Once more with spring's sweet growths are pied,
    I close each book, drop each pursuit,
And past the brook, no longer mute,
I joyous roam the countryside.

Look, here the violets shy abide
And there the mating robins hide—
    How keen my sense, how acute,
        When April's here!

And list! down where the shimmering tide
Hard by that farthest hill doth glide,
    Rise faint strains from shepherd's flute,
    Pan's pipes and Berecyntian lute.
Each sight, each sound fresh joys provide
        When April's here.

COURAGE! HE SAID

Ulysses, debarking in the Lotos Land,
Struck the one note that the hapless Ithacans
Travel-sick, mazed, bemused, could understand,
And understanding, follow.

"Courage," he said, "remember, is not Hope!"
He left the worn, safe ship, spume-stained and hollow.
"To be courageous is to face despair."
And through the groves and 'thwart the ambient air
Resounded reedy echoes:
"Face despair!"

But this they understood.
And plunging on prepared for best, and most prepared
For worst, found only in their stride
A deep umbrageous wood,
And grassy plains where they disported; eased
And bathed lame feet within a purling stream
And murmured: "Here, Odysseus, would we fain abide!"

But neither the stream's sweet ease

Nor the shade of the vast beech-trees,
Nor the blessed sense
Of the sweet, sweet soil
Beneath feet salt-cracked and worn
Brought to them even then,
(Still fainting and frayed and forlorn),
Such complete recompense
As the knowledge that once again
Facing the new and untried,
They had kept the courage of men!

STARS IN ALABAMA

In Alabama
Stars hang down so low,
So low they purge the soul
With their infinity.
Beneath their holy glance
Essential good
Rises to mingle with them
In that skiey sea.

At noon
Within the sandy cotton-field
Beyond the clay, red road
Bordered with green,
A Negro lad and lass
Cling hand in hand,
And Passion, hot-eyed, hot-lipped,
Lurks unseen.

But in the evening
When the skies lean down,
He's but a wistful boy,

A saintly maiden she.
For Alabama stars
Hang down so low,
So low they purge the soul
With their infinity.

HERE'S APRIL

I

This town that yesterday was dark and mean,
    And dank and raw with Winter's freezing air,
Is Light itself today, and verdant Sheen
    Gold-tinted, and besprent with perfume rare;
Translated over night to a parterre
    That makes me dream of Araby and Spain,
And all the healing places of the Earth,
    Where one lays by his woe, his bitter pain,—
        For peace and mirth.

II

Old Winter that stayed by us black and drear,
    And laid his blighting seal on everything,
Is vanished.—Is it true he once was here?—
    Mark how the ash-trees bud, and children sing,
And birds set up a faint, shy jargoning;
    And healing balm pours out from bole and leaf.

For Spring—sweet April's here in tree and grass!
 Oh foolish heart to fret so with your grief!
  This too shall pass!

DILWORTH ROAD REVISITED

The little road to Dilworth Town
  Still laughs and loiters by the brook,
And lovers love it in the Spring
  And haunt each blossomy nook.

Sad years ago my love and I
  Strolled all its sunny length one day,
To Dilworth's ivied church,—and then
  Sighing, we turned away.

Ah, Dilworth Road, can you still laugh
  When on another road's expanse,—
"The Ladies' Road", they call it,—lies
  My lover,—dead for France!

DOUCE SOUVENANCE

Again, as always, when the shadows fall,
　In that sweet space between the dark and day,
I leave the present and its fretful claims
　And seek the dim past where my memories stay.
I dream an old, forgotten, far-off dream,
　And think old thoughts and live old scenes anew,
Till suddenly I reach the heart of Spring—
　The spring that brought me you!
I see again a little woody lane,
　The moonlight rifting golden through the trees;
I hear the plaintive chirp of drowsy bird
　Lulled dreamward by a tender, vagrant breeze;
I hold your hand, I look into your eyes,
　I touch your lips,—oh, peerless, matchless dower!
Oh, Memory thwarting Time and Space and Death!
　Oh, Little Perfect Hour!

AGAIN IT IS SEPTEMBER

ILLUSTRATED BY LAURA WHEELER

Again it is September!
It seems so strange that I who made no vows
Should sit here desolate this golden weather
  And wistfully remember—

  A sigh of deepest yearning,
A glowing look and words that knew no bounds,
A swift response, an instant glad surrender
  To kisses wild and burning!

  Ay me!
  Again it is September!
It seems so strange that I who kept those vows
Should sit here lone, and spent, and mutely praying
  That I may not remember!

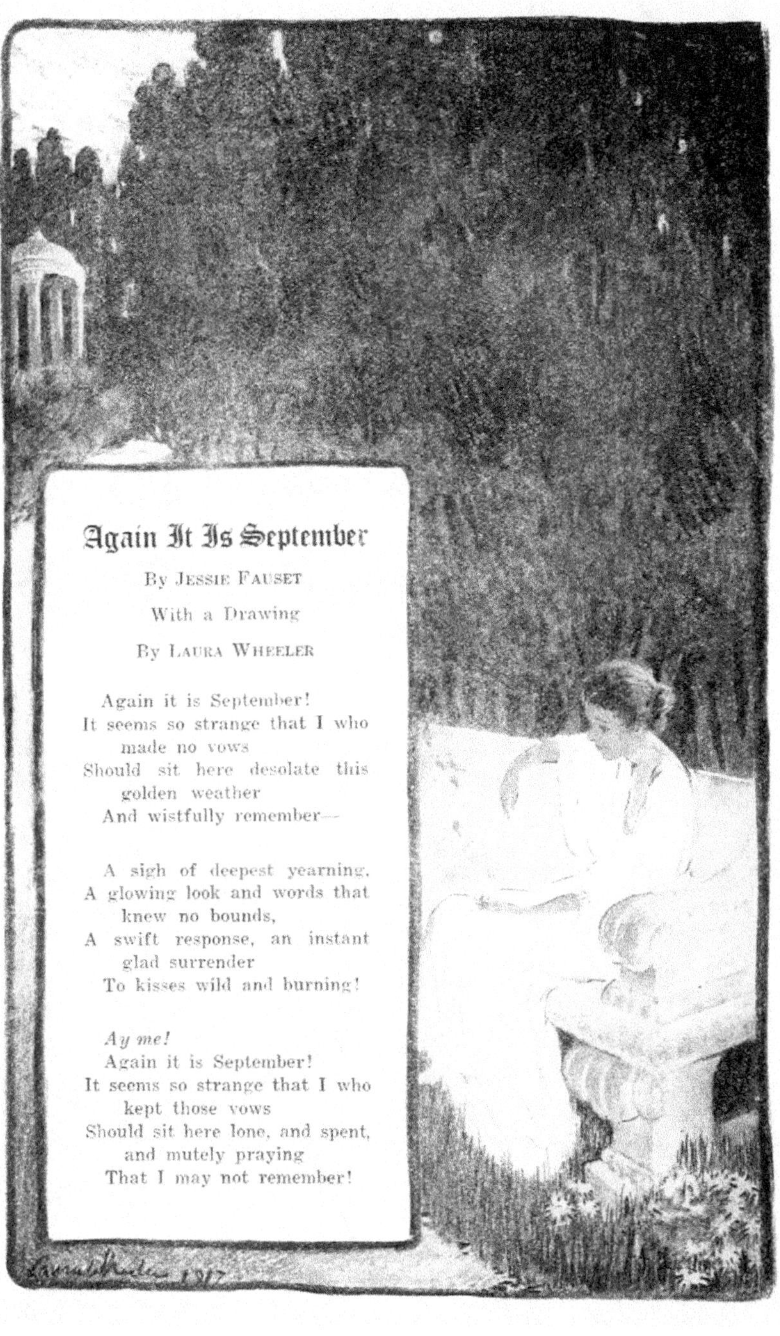

Again It Is September

By Jessie Fauset

With a Drawing

By Laura Wheeler

Again it is September!
It seems so strange that I who
made no vows
Should sit here desolate this
golden weather
And wistfully remember—

A sigh of deepest yearning,
A glowing look and words that
knew no bounds,
A swift response, an instant
glad surrender
To kisses wild and burning!

Ay me!
Again it is September!
It seems so strange that I who
kept those vows
Should sit here lone, and spent,
and mutely praying
That I may not remember!

POEMS FOR CHILDREN

DEDICATION

To Children, who with eager look
Scanned vainly library shelf and nook,
For History or Song or Story
That told of Colored Peoples' glory,—
We dedicate THE BROWNIES' BOOK.

AFTER SCHOOL

ILLUSTRATED BY LAURA WHEELER

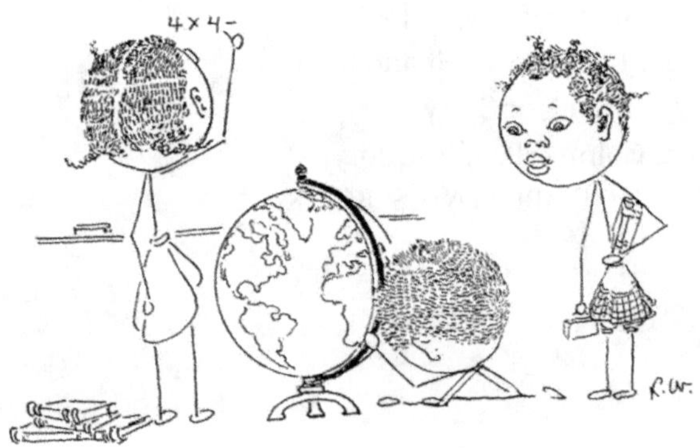

At nine o'clock I always say,
"I wish there'd be no school today."
And while the rest are at their books,
I give the teacher horrid looks,—
And think, "The minute school is over,
I'll race and romp with Ted Moore's Rover."
No matter what the teacher's saying,
My mind is off somewhere else playing.
But don't you know when Home-time comes,

I think, "I'll stay and work my sums.
I'll do 'four times four' on the board,
Or write how much wood makes a cord."

And Billy Hughes is just like me,
He stays back just as regularly!
He's always hunting out strange places
Upon the globe, and then he traces
A map with towns and states and mountains,
And public parks with trees and fountains!
And this is what's so queer to me—
Bill just *can't get* geography
In school-time, and I'm awful dumb,
I cannot do one single sum.
But just let that old teacher go—
There's nothing Bill and me don't know!

"Ted Moore's Rover"

THAT STORY OF GEORGE WASHINGTON

He did it with his little hatchet,
And just because he didn't catch it,
We write the theme in prose and verse,
And year by year we it rehearse.

Says Young America forsooth,
With all the logic wise of youth,
"If I, like George, cut down a tree,
I shall be like George, Q.E.D.

"If I like George am,"—thought heaven-sent—
"Then I, too, shall be President."
And so, like George, he plies his hatchet;
The difference is—*George didn't catch it*!

AT THE ZOO

ILLUSTRATED BY HILDA RUE WILKINSON

My mother said to me, "Now, mind,
To animals be always kind;
To every creature, bird or beast,
Show courtesy, to say the least!"
And then she took me to the Zoo,
(She said she'd nothing else to do,)
And showed me beasts of many styles,
From prairie dogs to crocodiles,
And take it from me, when I say
I didn't feel like getting gay,
Or doing them a bit of harm.
I wouldn't touch them for a farm.

AT THE ZOO

The lion was the first I saw,
I just looked at his awful paw
And thought, "I'll never trouble you."
I thought that of the tiger, too;
He was a handsome looking fellow.
And striped all black and real bright yellow.
But I could never play with him,
His look just made my poor head swim.

The elephant—they called him "Dunk,"
Looked mild, but had a squirmy trunk.
The panther and the wolf and bear,
Threw into me an awful scare.
(The bear looked pretty good, 'tis true.
But s'pose he started hugging you!)
The foxes didn't need their labels—
I'd read of *them* in *Aesop's Fables*!

The hippopotamus and his friend,
Rhinoceros, stood my hair on end.

The python and the anaconda,
Just made me grow of kindness, fonder.

I might have liked the dromedary—
But oh, his manner was so airy!
And, too, I fancied the giraffe,
His long neck really made me laugh.
My mother said, "Come see the birds,
They're just too nice and sweet for words."
She showed me, first, a horned owl—

That really is an awful fowl!
He blinked at me, as though to say,
"I'll bite your fingers. Get away!"
And then I say a pelican,
With long, sharp duck-bill. Well, he can
Be sure I'll never trouble him,
And where he swims, I'll never swim.

And next I saw a cassowary,
Who looked to me a bit contrary,
"Of bird and beast, I've had my fill,"
I said, "Please take me home, I'm ill.
I promise to take your advice,
You'll never have to tell me twice."
But after I was home, in bed,
I pulled the covers 'round my head,
And saw those creatures at the Zoo,
And thought, "No wonder that they're blue,
And look so cross and mean and mad,
They have enough to make them sad.
If I were locked up in a cage,
I'd just be in an awful rage.

Perhaps they've children far away,
Or friends who watch for them each day;
Perhaps they dream at night, they're free
In forests green and shadowy;
And then they wake to dull despair,—
And little boys who poke and stare.
Right then and there, I charged my mind,
To be to all God's creatures kind.
And kind to them I'll surely be
If only they'll be kind to me!

THE EASTER IDYL

ILLUSTRATED BY LAURA WHEELER

The Christ that was, like us a child
On Christmas long ago,
Grew up gentle lad and mild,—
They say twas wondrous when He smiled!—
And how His mother watched Him grow
So pure, so undefiled!

The Christ that was so kind and good
Had enemies, a host;
Though some there were that understood
And worshipped Him as people should,
The ones He thought would love him most,
Did all the ill they could.

THE
EASTER IDYL
by
Jessie Fauset
The Christ that was, like us a child
On Christmas long ago,
Grew up a gentle lad and mild,—
They say 'twas wondrous when He smiled!
And how His mother watched Him grow
So pure so undefiled!
The Christ that was so kind and good
Had enemies, a host;
Though some there were that understood
And worshipped Him as people should,
The ones He thought would love him most,
Did all the ill they could.

The Christ that was so meek and true
Was nailed upon a tree;
With horrid pikes they pierced Him through
And gave him vinegar and rue.
"Forgive them, Father," murmured He
"They know not what they do."
The Christ that hung on Calvary dead
Lay three days in the ground.
On Sabbath morn His mother sped
To watch beside his stony bed,
And heard the angel's voice resound,
"He's risen as He said!"
The Christ that was so lowly born
Now reigns, a Prince, above
His brow still wears the mark of thorn,
His hands are scarred—they were so torn—
But children peal their thanks and love
To Him, each Easter morn!

SPRING SONGS

ILLUSTRATED BY ALBERT K. SMITH

The Runaway Kite

The Runaway Kite
My kite broke loose on a windy day,
And 'way, 'way up in the air it flew;
And though I've sought for it, far and near,
It has never come back from the lofty blue.
Now where does it stay, and what does it see,
And what all day long does it find to do?

I think that it floats on a snowy cloud
Or jauntily rides on a saucy breeze;
And when it gets weary it flutters down
To the shelter of tall and stately trees;
Or the fairies may use it as a sail
For their fairy barks that patrol the seas.

The Singing Top

On sunny days I spin my top
From morning until noon;
It whirls in rings,
And hums and sings
This little pleasant tune,—
"Sweet April comes, then leafy May,
And then comes golden June!"

The Teasing Hoop

My hoop goes trundling down the street
   And I go skipping after,
And as it bounds along so fleet,
   It says with elfin laughter:
"Make up your mind that in this race
   You're bound to have the second place,
No matter, child, how hard you try,
   You cannot run as fast as I."

"Salt! Vinegar! Mustard!"

Spring evenings after supper
When we're all dressed up so neat,
We children take our skipping-rope
And play out in the street.
You never heard such noise and mirth,
   Or saw such nimble feet.

We jump all sorts of fancy ways,—
"High water, water low",
And some of us jump "Double Dutch",—
We do it fast or slow;
But "Vinegar, mustard, pepper, salt!"
   Is the favorite, you know.

Adventures on Roller Skates

On April afternoons I say,
  "Mama, I'd like to skate today."
She thinks I'll play out in the street
With Maude and Harold Jones and Pete,—
  But really I go far away.

Sometimes I skate in Switzerland,
  With ice-clad hills on every hand;
Sometimes I'm off in Russia far,—
(They still talk there about the czar!)
  I'm *never* here, you understand!

I skate in Greenland; Norway, too,
  And skim its fiords of icy blue.
When I get back my mother calls,
"Come in before the dampness falls!"
  She'd wonder if she really knew!

The Happy Organ Grinder

The organ man comes down our street
   On afternoons of later May,
And just as soon as he appears,
   I actually forget to play.
He is a ragged man and old,
   His day's work ought to make him weary;
And yet he smiles and smiles at me
   And always seems so bright and cheery.

   Perhaps his organ keeps him so,—
He makes it play such glorious things!
   And when he sees me listening there
He throws his gray head back and sings.
   His song excites me, makes me know
I'm listening to some thrilling story.
   My brother says the words are these,—
"Frenchmen, arise, awake to glory!"

TWO CHRISTMAS SONGS

I. The Crescent Moon

Last night I saw a crescent moon
Hang slimly silver in the sky;
A white cloud floated very near,
A star of gold was hovering by.
I watched and watched them through the night
And wished they were not hung so high.

I think the moon a cradle was
In which the little Lord lay sleeping;
The cloud a downy, fleecy quilt
Kept chill and cold from near Him creeping;
The star, a golden angel's eye,
Was watch and ward above Him keeping.

II. Christmas Eve

On Christmas Eve I lie awake
Far, far, I'm sure, into the night,

And watch until a golden star
Floods all my little room with light.
Some shepherds in the days of old
Watched, just like me, that star of gold.

And as I lie there in the gloom
I tell myself the Christmas story,
And how the little Savior Christ
Forsook for us His state and glory,
And came a little, lovely child
To save the earth, so sin-defiled.

And bye and bye my rooms grow vast,
The golden star shines close and clearer;
And music that seemed far and faint,
Drifts in about me near and nearer.
The bells in myriad churches ring,
And, *Hark! the Herald Angels sing!*

TRANSLATED POEMS

OBLIVION

FROM THE FRENCH OF MASSILLON COICOU (HAITI)

I hope when I am dead that I shall lie
In some deserted grave—I cannot tell you why,
But I should like to sleep in some neglected spot,
Unknown to every one, by every one forgot.

There lying I should taste with my dead breath
The utter lack of life, the fullest sense of death;
And I should never hear the note of jealousy or hate,
The tribute paid by passers-by to tombs of state.

To me would never penetrate the prayers and tears
That futilely bring torture to dead and dying ears;
There I should lie annihilate and my dead heart would bless
Oblivion—the shroud and envelope of happiness.

THE POOL

FROM THE FRENCH OF AMÉDÉE BRUN (HAITI)

The lonely pool sleeps in the depth of the glade
At the foot of a slope which its beauty discloses;
And the whispering reeds make a rustling retreat
Which the stream lips or leaves as it wakes or reposes.

The heather erects a dense rampart of green
To conceal the sweet tide which reflects in its deeps
The tops of tall trees, and this one labor done,
Forgetting aught else, dreams and placidly sleeps.

Now and then comes a bird—a blackcap or a swallow,
Which with its swift flight makes the mute, formless hollow
Of solitude ring with a shrill, plaintive sound.

Its wings barely skim the pool drowsy with slumber,
Yet small, eager waves circling wide, without number,
Haste to die 'mid the pitying reeds grouped around.

TO A FOREIGN MAID

FROM THE FRENCH OF OSWALD DURAND (HAITI)

For one glance from those eyes
   Of such heavenly blue
   Than they rival the skies,—
   My life' forfeit to you.
   But that's a small prize—
   Do you not think so Rose?
   Not enough I suppose
For a glance from those eyes!

For a curl from your brow
   Of that hair soft and fine,
   Gold as gold corn I trow—
   I would give my divine
   Hope of heav'n. A poor vow!
   Do you not think so Rose?
   Not enough I suppose
For a curl from your brow!

For a little fleet kiss
   From your lips Cupidwise
   Where *l'Amour* laughs in bliss,

I'd renounce family ties.
Even so I'm remiss—
Do you not think so Rose?
Not enough to propose
For a little fleet kiss!

For your love chaste and white
I'd let slip from my hand,
Heaven, life, family right,
—And the dear Fatherland!
Ah! I sigh at my plight!
Do you not think dear Rose,
That's too much to propose
For your love chaste and white?

THE SUN OF BRITTAINY

TRANSLATED FROM THE FRENCH

I

"The sea compels me; sister I must go.
Nay! Do not hold me,—I'm of age you know!
I am a Breton and of noble birth.
The pathway of the ocean draws me so!"

"But, brother, if you leave, what good am I on earth?
Without you, dear, my life is poor and cold.
Ah! stir not from our fold!
Remain with me until we both are old!
Our mountain life is happy, brother dear.
And then in Brittainy the sunlight is so clear!"

II

"Upon a vessel which shall bear your name
A captain I'll return, but still the same.
Within three years we'll own these woods, this land;
And lords of all we'll be, and all will claim."

"But think," said she, "what more can you demand?
Our cottage rises from the earth's brown mold,
And happy, happy is our humble fold.
Remain with me until we both are old!
Our mountain life is happy, brother dear,
And then in Brittainy the sunlight is so clear!"

III

But he must leave her though the heavens fall.
Ten lonely years—no word from him no call!
Beside the hearth his sister, his best friend,
Wept, constant, wearing sorrow as a pall.
Then suddenly her grief comes to an end.
One day a sailor, shipwrecked, racked with cold,
Sought shelter.
"You! My brother, grown so old!"
"Yes, sister mine, I've come back to the fold.
This mountain life will heal my suffering drear.
And sweetest Brittainy, thy sunlight is so clear!"

NOTES

Introduction

1. Shockley, Ann Allen. *Afro-American Women Writers, 1746-1933: An Anthology and Critical Guide*. G.K. Hall, 1988. "According to Fauset biographer Carolyn Wedin Sylvander, 'Jessie "Redmona" Fauset was born 27 April 1882 in Camden County, Snow Hill Center Township, New Jersey.' ... Joseph J. Feeney, S. J. who has also sought to set the record straight, identified 26 April 1882 as the correct date and Frederickville, Camden County, as the place. Both Sylvander and Feeney used the Fauset family Bible for documentation. The discrepancy between the two as to place is accounted for by Feeney's quoting the librarian of Camden County, who noted that in 1882 Frederickville was part of Snow Hill, New Jersey, a community of freed slaves."
2. Sylvander, Carolyn Wedin. *Jessie Redmon Fauset, Black American Writer*. Whitstone Publishing Company, 1981.
3. Du Bois, W. E. B. *The Brownies' book*. New York, N.Y.: Du Bois and Dill, to 1921, 1920. Periodical. Retrieved from the Library of Congress. <www.loc.gov/item/22001351/>
4. "Impressions of the Second Pan-African Congress." *The Crisis*. Nov 1921, pp. 12-18.
5. "What Europe Thought of the Pan-African Congress." *The Crisis*, Dec 1921, pp. 60-67.
6. National Archives and Records Administration (NARA); Washington D.C.; NARA Series: Passport Applications, January 2, 1906 - March 31, 1925; Roll #: 1716; Volume #: Roll 1716 - Certificates: 75000-75375, 16 Aug 1921-16 Aug 1921
7. Wall, Cheryl A.. *Women of the Harlem Renaissance*. Indiana University Press, 1995.
8. Hughes, Langston. *The Big Sea, an Autobiography*. Hill and Wang, 1963, p. 218.
9. Locke, Alain. "Foreword." *The New Negro: An Interpretation*. A. and C. Boni, 1925. p. XXVI.
10. Fauset's essays about her European travels, 1925-1926: "Yarrow Revisited," "This Way to the Flea Market," Parts I and II of "Dark Algiers the White," and "The Eucalyptus Tree."
11. Lewis, David L.. *When Harlem Was in Vogue*. Penguin Publishing Group, 1997, pp. 198-199
12. Sylvander, Carolyn Wedin. "Jessie Redmon Fauset." *Dictionary of Literary Biographies Vol. 51. Afro-American Writers from the Harlem Renaissance to 1940*. Gale Research Company, 1987.
13. Shockley, Ann Allen. *Afro-American Women Writers, 1746-1933: An Anthology and Critical Guide*. G.K. Hall, 1988.
14. Hughes, Langston. *The Big Sea: An Autobiography*. Hill and Wang, 1963.
15. "The Opportunity Dinner: An Impression." *Opportunity: A Journal of Negro Life*, Jul 1927, p. 208.
16. "Harris-Fauset Wedding." *The New Age*, New York, New York. Apr 13, 1929, p. 2.
17. Harris-Fauset wedding guests included Fauset's siblings, Helen Fauset Lanning, Marion Fauset, Earl Huff, Redmon Fauset Jr., and Arthur Huff Fauset. Also in attendance were Sadie Mossell Alexander, Regina Anderson Andrews, Eva D. Bowles, Nellie Bright, Helen Curtis, W.E.B. Du Bois, Augustus Granville Dill, Margaret Smith Douglas, Robert Douglass, Robert J. Elzy, T. Thomas Fortune, Hallie Queen Jackson,

Brenda Moryck, Godfrey Nurse, Arthur Spingarn, Helen Hagan Williams, and William H. Wortham.

18. "Jessie Fauset, Noted Negro Writer, Dies." *The Montclair Times*, Montclair, New Jersey. May 4, 1961, p. 6.
19. Levine, Karen Rae. "Survey of Short Stories by Women of the Harlem Renaissance Published in Comprehensive Academic Anthologies, 1991-2018," Independent Study, 2023.
20. Johnson, Abby Arthur. "Literary Midwife: Jessie Redmon Fauset." *Phylon*, 2nd Qtr., 1978, Vol. 39, No. 2.
21. Sylvander, Carolyn Wedin. *Jessie Redmon Fauset, Black American Writer*. Whitstone Publishing Company, 1981.
22. Garcia, Claire Oberon. "Jessie Redmon Fauset, Reconsidered." *The Harlem Renaissance Revisited: Politics, Arts, and Letters*. Johns Hopkins University Press, 2010.
23. Jenkins, Morgan. "The Forgotten Work of Jessie Redmon Fauset." *The New Yorker*, February 18, 2017. https://www.newyorker.com/books/page-turner/the-forgotten-work-of-jessie-redmon-fauset
24. Lewis, David L.. *When Harlem Was in Vogue*. Penguin Publishing Group, 1997, 121.

WOMEN OF THE HARLEM RENAISSANCE ANTHOLOGY SERIES TITLES

SHORT-TAKE ANTHOLOGIES

ON BEING COLORED ME: Reflections on Race and Gender by Women of the Harlem Renaissance

CROSSING THE COLOR LINE: Short Fiction on Passing by Women of the Harlem Renaissance

HARLEM ON HER MIND: Prose, Poems & Plays by Women of the Harlem Renaissance

PRIZE POEMS BY WOMEN OF THE HARLEM RENAISSANCE

POEMS BY BOSTON'S WOMEN OF THE HARLEM RENAISSANCE

RONDEAU: The Collected Poems of Jessie Redmon Fauset

HOW BRIGHT THE FLAME: The Collected Poems of Mae V. Cowdery, 1927-1935

EXPANDED ANTHOLOGIES

FAITHFULLY YOURS, JESSIE REDMON FAUSET: Stories, Poems & Personal Essays

ESSENTIAL SHORT STORIES BY WOMEN OF THE HARLEM RENAISSANCE: Volumes 1 & 2

THE SATURDAY EVENING QUILL: Stories, Poems & Plays by Boston's Women of the Harlem Renaissance

VOICES RESTORED: The Performance Edition

(A companion anthology of poems performed at a spoken word event)

www.ingramcontent.com/pod-product-compliance
Lightning Source LLC
Chambersburg PA
CBHW070545120726
47909CB00007B/2241

* 9 7 9 8 9 9 2 3 0 7 5 1 1 *